MURDLE Jr.

CURIOUS CRIMES FOR CURIOUS MINDS

MURDLE Jr.

CURIOUS CRIMES FOR CURIOUS MINDS

Solve Your Way Through

40

Puzzle Mysteries!

G. T. KARBER

LITTLE, BROWN AND COMPANY

New York Boston

Little, Brown and Company
Hachette Book Group
1290 Avenue of the Americas, New York, NY 10104
Visit us at LBYR.com

First Edition: November 2024

Little, Brown and Company is a division of Hachette Book Group, Inc.
The Little, Brown name and logo are registered trademarks of Hachette Book Group, Inc.

The publisher is not responsible for websites
(or their content) that are not owned by the publisher.

Little, Brown and Company books may be purchased in bulk for business,
educational, or promotional use. For information, please contact your local bookseller or
the Hachette Book Group Special Markets Department at special.markets@hbgusa.com.

Library of Congress Cataloging-in-Publication Data
Names: Karber, G. T., author.
Title: Murdle Jr. : curious crimes for curious minds :
solve your way through 40 puzzle mysteries! / G. T. Karber.
Other titles: Curious crimes for curious minds
Description: First edition. | New York, NY : Little, Brown and Company, [2024] | Summary: "Based
on the internationally bestselling Murdle puzzle books, Murdle Jr. is an introduction to puzzle-solving
for kids, with over forty mysteries featuring clues, maps, mazes, and more."
—Provided by publisher.
Identifiers: LCCN 2024017161 | ISBN 9780316582551 (paperback)
Subjects: LCSH: Puzzles. | Detective and mystery stories. | Riddles. | Lateral thinking puzzles.
Classification: LCC GV1507.D4 K38 2024 | DDC 793.73—dc23/eng/20240506
LC record available at https://lccn.loc.gov/2024017161

ISBNs: 978-0-316-58255-1 (trade paperback), 978-0-316-58620-7 (Barnes & Noble)

Printed in Indiana, USA

LSC-C, 01/25

Printing 3, 2024

For Reya

CONTENTS

HOW TO SOLVE

THE FOUR JUNIOR DETECTIVES STOOD AT THE ENTRANCE TO Castle Eminence, staring into the empty darkness ahead of them. They had traveled through the Screaming Forest and the Madding Mountains, but still, the depths of this castle terrified them.

"The chance of this going well for us is minuscule," said Olivia. She always knew facts like that, and used words like *minuscule* when saying *very small* would do.

Julius agreed. "I don't know about the odds, but this place gives me bad vibes." And he was famous for his vast knowledge of vibes, or at least his ability to feel them.

"Of course it gives you bad vibes!" exclaimed Jake. She was the tough talker of the group, easily able to intimidate her way through school. "It's a super-spooky castle atop terrifying mountains above a haunted forest! But we can't let fear stop us. We're detectives now."

"Technically, *junior* detectives," Olivia corrected.

"Well, either way. It's our case. And we can't go back and say we were too scared to even go inside."

But it was Buster McPaws, the world's greatest detective (in the cat category, at least), who was the first of them to walk into Castle Eminence. He strode inside with the confidence of a creature who knew that nothing could harm him, since he still had seven lives remaining.

After the cat had led the way, the rest of them felt pretty silly standing at the door, so they snuck in behind their furry leader.

"Now," said Julius, "remind me why we're doing this again."

Olivia answered him. "The Detective Club assigned us a simple case: Figure out who is hiding in this castle, find where they are hiding, and uncover their evil plans."

"Oh," Julius said. "I meant why we felt this was a good idea."

Olivia continued, ignoring him. "Analysis of this structure suggests that at least three suspects are currently inside it. Based on my calculations, they are these three…"

WHO IS INSIDE THE CASTLE?

VISCOUNT EMINENCE

Apparently, it's pronounced VIE-COUNT. He's older than his father, and he outlived all his sons.

(5'2" • LEFT-HANDED • GRAY EYES • BROWN HAIR)

MAJOR RED

Major Red is a revolutionary leader who is loved by some people and feared by many more.

(6'2" • LEFT-HANDED • BROWN EYES • BROWN HAIR)

AGENT APRICOT

She's a representative from S.P.Y., a secret society dedicated to secret plans.

(5'7" • RIGHT-HANDED • GREEN EYES • BLACK HAIR)

Once the junior detectives were inside, they crept around together—as a team—careful not to employ the absolutely ridiculous strategy of splitting up, and they discovered that there were three places where their suspects might still be hiding out.

WHERE ARE THEY?

THE GREAT HALL

High ceilings, a giant table, an enormous framed portrait of Viscount Eminence.

THE TOWER

It has a great view of the haunted forest below, and no place to run!

THE DUNGEON

If you split up to search the castle, this is the place you want to search least.

And finally, the four junior detectives knew that each of these three suspects had their own specific secret plans, and that each of them had a different hidden agenda.

WHAT ARE THEIR SECRET PLANS?

TO TAKE OVER THE WORLD

This is a pretty classic supervillain plot. You can't blame one for trying.

TO GET REALLY, REALLY RICH

A lot of people have these plans, but only supervillains succeed at them!

TO GO ON VACATION

Honestly, if these are your secret plans, you should probably be allowed to pursue them.

"All right, that's enough research," Jake said. "Now it's time to look at the actual clues we can use to crack this case wide open."

The four of them put their heads together and made a list of the clues and evidence that they absolutely, positively knew for sure.

CLUES & EVIDENCE

Because of his enormous ego, Major Red would hide out only in the Great Hall.

The shortest suspect was not in the tower.

The person in the dungeon just wanted to go on vacation.

The person in the tower did not want to get rich.

They were here to find the culprit who wanted to take over the world.

"So," Olivia said, "each of these suspects would be hiding in one of these places, and each would have one of these plans. First we'll have to figure out who would have which plan and be in which hiding spot, and then we can determine which one of them is trying to conquer the world."

"We get it, Olivia," Jake said.

"But just in case we don't," Julius said, "maybe walk us through it."

"Okay, so, first, we've got to use a Deduction Grid." She drew one in her Detective Notebook. "Each of these boxes represents a connection between two things. For example, I drew an arrow to the box that represents Viscount Eminence being in the dungeon, to help you all understand." (See Figure 1.)

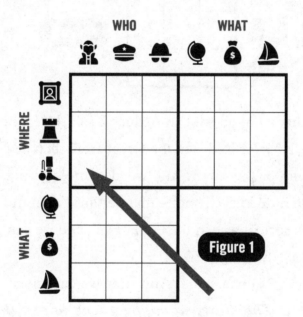

Figure 1

Julius looked at her drawing and said, "I knew that," but he wasn't very convincing.

"Now we'll use this to work through the clues, one at a time. The first clue is simple enough: *Because of his enormous ego, Major Red would hide out only in the Great Hall.*

We'll use a check mark in the Deduction Grid to show that Major Red would be in the Great Hall." (See Figure 2.)

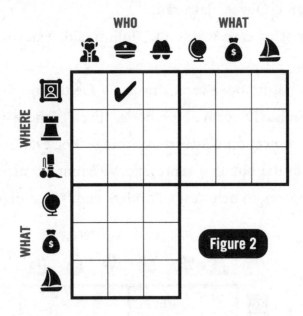

Figure 2

"But that's not all we can deduce," said Jake, "because we know that if Major Red is in the Great Hall, then he can't be in the dungeon or the tower. And we also know—since only one person can hide in each spot—that neither Viscount Eminence nor Agent Apricot was in the Great Hall, and we can put *X*s in their boxes." (See Figure 3.)

"Correct," Olivia said. "And now we can move on to the second clue: ***The shortest suspect was not in the tower.*** Looking at the statistics we've put together, we can tell that Viscount Eminence is the shortest suspect, so we can put an *X* in the box where the tower and Viscount Eminence intersect."

"And there's more!" said Jake. "Because now we know that

if the viscount isn't in the tower, and he's not in the Great Hall, then he must be in the dungeon. And we've figured out the hiding places for everyone!" (See Figure 4.)

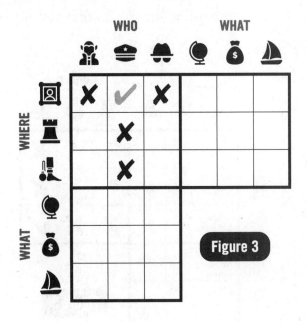

Figure 3

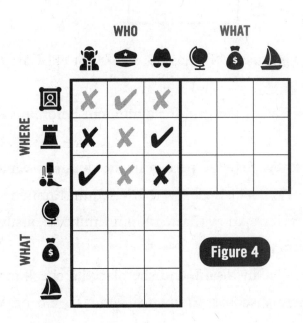

Figure 4

"But now we've got to figure out their plans," Olivia said. "Our third clue: ***The person in the dungeon just wanted to go on vacation.*** So we can put a check mark where those two intersect, and *X*s in the other squares in that row and column." (See Figure 5.)

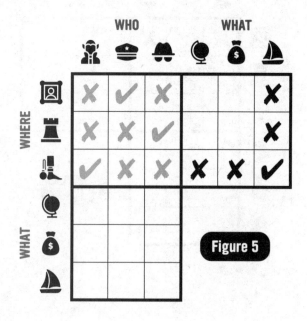

Figure 5

Olivia continued, "But again, that's not all! Can you figure out what else?"

Julius stared at the grid for a moment before his eyes went wide.

"If we know that the person in the dungeon wanted to go on vacation, and we also know that Viscount Eminence is in the dungeon, then we know that Viscount Eminence just wanted to go on vacation!"

"Correct!" Olivia said, and she placed a check mark in the square where Viscount Eminence and "To Go on Vacation" intersected. And then put *X*s in the other squares in that row and column. (See Figure 6.)

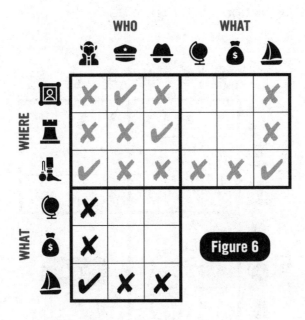

Figure 6

"Now we can move on to the next clue: ***The person in the tower did not want to get rich***. So, you know what to do now: We put an *X* in the box where getting rich and the tower intersect." (See Figure 7.)

"And that means," Jake said, "we know that the person in the Great Hall wanted to

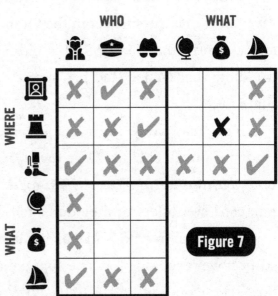

Figure 7

get rich. And we know that the person in the tower wanted to take over the world." She added the check marks and the *X* to complete that section. (See Figure 8.)

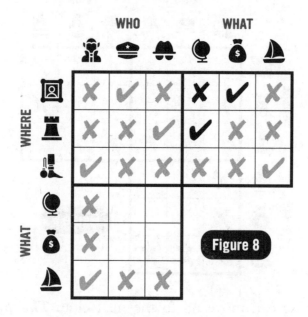

Figure 8

"But we can still make more deductions!" Olivia replied. "We know that the suspect in the Great Hall wants to get rich, and we know that Major Red is hiding in the Great Hall, so we know that Major Red has secret plans to get rich." (See Figure 9.)

"Now that we've filled out the Deduction Grid, we are ready for our final clue: ***They were here to find the culprit who wanted to take over the world.*** These clues on a separate card are different; they don't tell us anything about who has which plan or who is in which location—they tell us which suspect we're looking for. The supervillain we're here to investigate is the one with plans to take over the world."

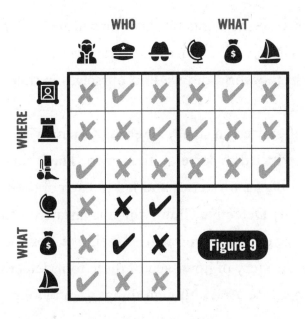

Figure 9

"And we know that Agent Apricot wants to take over the world!" Julius exclaimed.

So the four detectives (led by the courageous Buster McPaws) raced to the top of the tower, where, sure enough, they found Agent Apricot standing on the balcony and looking out over the Screaming Forest below.

"We've got you!" they exclaimed.

But Agent Apricot turned around with a smile.

"No, detectives," she said. "You may have *found* me, but I believe you will find that it is *I* who have *you*. Guards!"

Suddenly, a small army of guards appeared behind the four detectives.

"Throw them in the dungeon," Agent Apricot ordered.

And despite their best efforts (and the claws of Buster Mc-Paws), the four junior detectives were captured, tied up, and carried down to the dungeon. Jake turned to Buster and said, "You just had to be the brave one, didn't you?"

"How in the world did we find ourselves in this mess?" Julius wondered.

It had all started so small, for each of them, with a tiny mystery they had tried to solve on their own. These tiny mysteries turned into bigger mysteries and led to each of them being recruited by the Detective Club (which is always on the lookout for promising detectives, no matter their age...or species!).

This is the story of how each of these four detectives solved their first big case. And although things aren't looking great for them right now, with your help, they'll be able to escape the clutches of the evil Agent Apricot and foil her plans for world domination.

All you need are your wits, your determination, and a pencil.

Good luck, detective! We're counting on you.

WHERE TO START

THIS BOOK CONTAINS THE FIRST MAJOR MYSTERIES OF FOUR junior detectives. You can read about them in any order you want, but you should read all of them before they reunite for *Disaster at Detective Academy* (page 171).

If one of them interests you more than the others, feel free to start with them! If not, you can start with Jake and read straight through.

Jake the Gumshoe is a no-nonsense, in-your-face private eye. She goes to a stuck-up private school, but only because the public schools all kicked her out. She knows that sometimes the best way to figure out whodunit is to accuse everybody and see how they react.

Julius the Intuitive knows that sometimes you just know something, and you can't explain why. He'll follow his hunches, and he'll back them up with logic later. Sometimes the most important clue is in the stars or the marot cards, and you never know where any thread will lead.

Buster McPaws the Snoop has the most perceptive eye in the detective business. He can smell a crime from a mile away and a treat from ten. He loves food almost as much as he loves the thrill of the chase.

Olivia the Consultant is a real brainiac, potentially one of the smartest kids to ever live. She can hack a computer, calculate complex mathematical equations, and deduce whodunit without ever having to get her hands dirty.

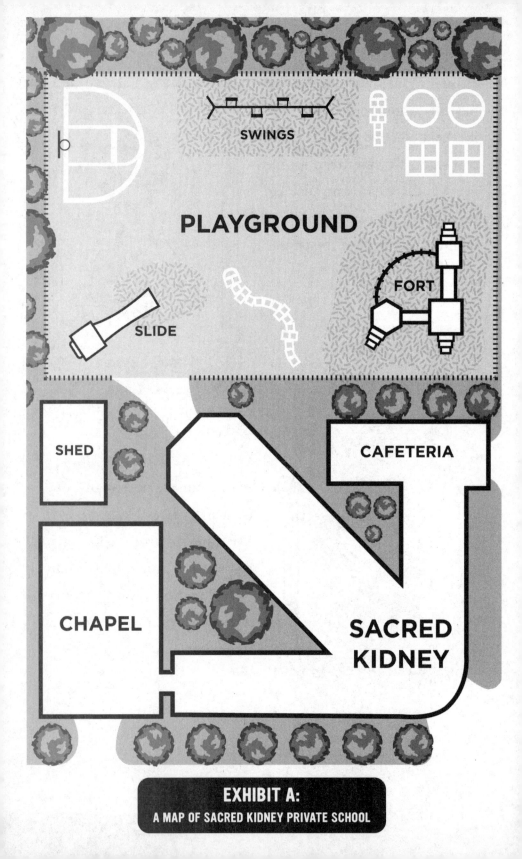

SWINGS

PLAYGROUND

SLIDE

FORT

SHED

CAFETERIA

CHAPEL

SACRED KIDNEY

EXHIBIT A:
A MAP OF SACRED KIDNEY PRIVATE SCHOOL

JAKE

IN

THE CASE OF THE MISSING PENCIL

JAKE WAS THE TOUGHEST KID AT HER SCHOOL, SACRED KIDNEY. She had been the toughest kid at her previous school, too, until she was kicked out after the event now known only as "the Pizza Day Disaster."

Jake swore she was innocent, but nobody believed her.

So that school kicked her out, and she got sent across town to Sacred Kidney, a private school run by the church. There, she'd struggled to fit in, not only socially, but also into her standard-issue polyester uniform. The only other kid she got along with was Sterling, her sidekick, although he preferred to be called her best friend. He was always getting into trouble, and she was always getting him out of it.

For example, one day during recess, Jake was chewing on a straw when Sterling ran up to her with tears in his eyes.

"Why are you crying?" Jake asked, partly because she wanted to know what was wrong, and partly because she didn't want people to see her sidekick cry. That didn't look tough.

"Somebody stole my *lucky* pencil!" Sterling cried.

"Could you describe it to me?"

"It's about this big, and it's brown, but it writes in rainbow colors. That's why it's so lucky!"

Jake wondered if it was the Sacred Kidney Cat Burglar.

All year, valuable items had been going missing from Sacred Kidney: a gold crown that had once been worn by a bishop, an anointed silver goblet, and more. Each time, Principal Apple-green had launched an investigation, and each time, nothing was found. Jake had looked into it, too. But the Cat was careful, and she left no clues behind. But this time, the Sacred Kidney Cat Burglar had made a huge mistake. They never should have stolen from Jake's sidekick.

"Dry your eyes, kiddo," she told him. "I'll find your missing pencil even if I have to turn this whole school upside down."

But Jake didn't know how far she would have to go to solve this case. She didn't understand that it was going to turn out to be the most difficult case she'd ever accepted, that it would lead straight to the top, and that it would change the very course of her life forever.

But it would.

This is *The Case of the Missing Pencil*.

YOU CAN'T SPELL *CRIME* WITHOUT A PENCIL

"Where was the last place you saw your lucky pencil?" Jake asked.

"Out here, during recess!" Sterling replied. "I left it balanced on the swings and went to check out some cool rocks over by the trees. By the time I got back, it was gone."

Figure out who was where during the crime, and you'll be able to determine whodunit.

WHO STOLE THE PENCIL?

ROSE

She's a ten-year-old chess prodigy who could probably beat your dad.

(4'4" • LEFT-HANDED • HAZEL EYES • BROWN HAIR)

DAISY

She's the most popular girl in class; nobody else even comes close.

(4'6" • RIGHT-HANDED • BLUE EYES • BLOND HAIR)

BRICK

Why would Brick steal a pencil? He hates doing homework. Maybe he wanted to stab somebody?

(4'7" • RIGHT-HANDED • BROWN EYES • BROWN HAIR)

Detectives! The solution to each mystery will appear upside down at the beginning of the next one. Don't flip ahead until you think you know who did it!

WHERE WERE THEY?

THE SLIDE

Stand in a line to climb up this slide, only to slide back down to where you started.

THE SWINGS

Jake thinks the swings are for wafflers: Pick a direction and stick to it.

THE FORT

The most strategically important place on the playground.

Brick was not anywhere near a line. He *hated* standing in lines.

The chess prodigy was at the place closest to the cafeteria. (See Exhibit A, at the beginning of this section!)

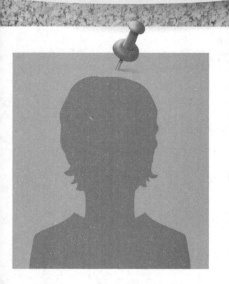

Jake figured whoever stole the pencil had to be by the swings.

HINT

Since Rose, the chess prodigy, was in the fort (the place closest to the school), and Brick was not by the slide (the only place with a line), that means Daisy had to be at the slide.

WHO

ROSE

DAISY

BRICK

WHERE

THE SLIDE

THE SWINGS

THE FORT

WHO?

WHERE?

THE WRITE WAY TO FIND A PENCIL

When the students made it back to the classroom, Jake confronted Brick at his desk. "What pencil?" he asked. "I don't have any pencil!" And he showed her his empty pockets. Jake knew he must have stashed the pencil somewhere in the classroom. Each location would require its own method to search. Match the locations with the methods, then discover where it must be hidden!

WHERE WAS THE PENCIL?

MISS SAFFRON'S DESK

It would be really bold to stash the pencil in Miss Saffron's desk.

(LARGE-SIZED)

BRICK'S CUBBY

Brick's cubby is the most disorganized place Jake has ever seen. And she's seen her own room.

(SMALL-SIZED)

THE FERRET CAGE

Miss Saffron kept a ferret as a pet in her room, which made class more exciting. But also smellier.

(MEDIUM-SIZED)

Solution to Episode One

"It was Brick, by the swings!"

Brick laughed. "You say I have it. I say I don't. Now what?" Jake was about to roll up her sleeves to show him *what*, but just then, the bell rang and the students were called inside. Jake would have to settle this in the classroom.

HOW WOULD JAKE SEARCH FOR IT?

CREATING A HUGE DISTRACTION

She wasn't exactly sure what the distraction would be, though. Maybe a stink bomb.

BEING REALLY QUIET AND SNEAKY

She called this the tiptoe method, and she had never once in her life done it.

LOUDLY CONFRONTING BRICK ABOUT IT

Just blurt out the whole thing and hope it all goes well, aka her usual strategy.

CLUES & EVIDENCE

The only real way to
check the large location would be
by creating a huge distraction.

Jake wrote a note in her notebook
using the Backward Code:
"I CAN'T SEARCH THE
FERRET CAGE BY
BEING REALLY
QUIET AND SNEAKY."

Jake knew she'd
have to use her usual
method to find the pencil.

HINT

To read the Backward Code, it's simple: Just hold it up to
a mirror!

MISS SAFFRON'S DESK

BRICK'S CUBBY

THE FERRET CAGE

HOW

**CREATING A HUGE
DISTRACTION**

**BEING REALLY
QUIET AND SNEAKY**

**LOUDLY CONFRONTING
BRICK ABOUT IT**

WHERE?

HOW?

THE MYSTERY UNFOLDS

Jake saw Brick smirk as she walked to the principal's office for disrupting class. And she still hadn't found the missing pencil! Where could it be? Suddenly, it dawned on her: He must have had an accomplice stash it on the way in from recess. But who helped him? And where would they put it?

WHO HID THE PENCIL FOR BRICK?

THE NEW JANITOR

He's got a big mustache, and even bigger eyebrows. He looks familiar, but Jake can't quite place him.

(6'0" • RIGHT-HANDED • BROWN EYES • BLACK HAIR)

COACH RASPBERRY JR.

Why would Coach Raspberry Jr. want to steal a pencil? Wouldn't a math coach have a ton of pencils?

(6'1" • RIGHT-HANDED • BLUE EYES • BLOND HAIR)

DAISY

Why would she risk her popularity for Brick? Maybe working with bullies is how she managed to get popular in the first place.

(4'6" • RIGHT-HANDED • BLUE EYES • BLOND HAIR)

SISTER LAPIS

In addition to being a sister for the Church, she's also the school librarian. Her habit is reading, so to speak.

(5'2" • RIGHT-HANDED • BROWN EYES • BROWN HAIR)

Solution to Episode Two

The pencil was in the ferret cage, and she'd have to loudly confront Brick about it!

And so she did.

"Brick stole a pencil and he hid it in the ferret cage!" she announced. She stormed over and started looking through the cage, the bedding, and the ferret food.

Not only did she not find the pencil, but she also really upset Miss Saffron, who said, "That's enough, Jake! Go to the principal's office!"

WHERE WOULD THEY HAVE STASHED IT?

THE DUMPSTER OUTSIDE

All they'd have to do is toss it in there. But how would they get it back out?

(SMELLS BAD)

THE TRASH CAN IN THE HALLWAY

It'd be a lot easier to retrieve the pencil from here, but a lot harder to hide it.

(SMELLS BAD)

THE PRINCIPAL'S OFFICE

Of course, this is the last place Jake would look, so it's a likely spot to find it.

(SMELLS OKAY)

THE JANITORIAL CLOSET

Mixed in with the soaps and mops and... wait, why is a magnifying glass in here?

(SMELLS LIKE BLEACH)

CLUES & EVIDENCE

Coach Raspberry Jr.
hadn't been anywhere near any
place that smelled bad.

Sister Lapis had been in
the last place Jake would look.

Daisy was not in or
around the dumpster.

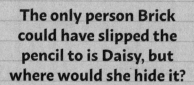

The only person Brick could have slipped the pencil to is Daisy, but where would she hide it?

HINT

The janitor wasn't in the janitor's closet all day! He was cleaning out the dumpster.

WHO

	 THE NEW JANITOR	 COACH RASPBERRY JR.	 DAISY	 SISTER LAPIS
 THE DUMPSTER OUTSIDE				
 THE TRASH CAN IN THE HALLWAY				
 THE PRINCIPAL'S OFFICE				
 THE JANITORIAL CLOSET				

WHERE

_____

WHO?

_____

WHERE?

EPISODE FOUR
THE GROSS CASE OF THE GARBAGE CAN

Sometimes being a detective was a dirty job, but Jake would do anything to crack a case. She knew the pencil was in the trash can. She was going to find it. No matter how dirty things got. Match the container with how deep it is in the trash can to find where the pencil is.

WHAT'S THE PENCIL HIDDEN INSIDE?

A USED TISSUE

This is the absolute grossest way to hide it.

(WET)

A MANILA ENVELOPE

Honestly, it would be great if it was in here and dry, but we both know that's not happening.

(DRY)

WRAPPED IN A BANANA PEEL

And it wasn't a new banana peel, either. It was pretty slimy.

(WET)

JUST LOOSE

The good part is that it would be easy to see. The bad part is that it would be touching everything else.

(DRY)

Solution to Episode Three

"It was Daisy, and she threw it in the trash can in the hallway!"

Fortunately, Jake had the perfect opportunity to search the trash can on the way to the principal's office. Then she could show up, pencil in hand, and make the case that it wasn't Jake who needed to be punished: It was Brick. Not that Jake cared about getting out of a punishment, exactly. She just wanted to see justice done.

HOW DEEP IN THE TRASH CAN IS IT?

SITTING ON THE TOP

What an ideal situation it would be if this was where it was.

SOMEWHERE IN THE MIDDLE

By this point of digging through the garbage, Jake had said goodbye to her mind.

BURIED ON THE BOTTOM

To dig all the way to the bottom, you have to get through a *lot* of garbage.

IT'S ACTUALLY *BEHIND* THE TRASH CAN

This is the last place Jake would look for garbage. But maybe it should be the first.

There was a manila envelope sitting on the top. So Jake checked there first, and it obviously wasn't there.

A banana peel was sitting somewhere in the middle, and Jake touched it. Gross.

Anything that was just loose would have been buried on the bottom.

Jake discovered the pencil in the last place she looked! Argh!

HINT

Here's a hint: Digging through the garbage is a bad idea in general.

WHAT

A USED TISSUE

A MANILA ENVELOPE

WRAPPED IN A BANANA PEEL

JUST LOOSE

WHERE

SITTING ON THE TOP

SOMEWHERE IN THE MIDDLE

BURIED ON THE BOTTOM

IT'S ACTUALLY *BEHIND* THE TRASH CAN

WHAT?

WHERE?

THE SENTENCING OF DETECTIVE JAKE

Sister Lapis tossed Jake into the tiny seat opposite Principal Applegreen, and Jake immediately said, "What am I being charged with, Principal?" The principal opened his mouth to reply, but then everybody began to talk at once. The principal struggled to follow what was going on. Why was Jake in trouble, and how serious was that crime?

WHAT IS THE CHARGE?

HANGING OUT IN THE HALLS

This is the rule that Jake breaks the most, but she calls it "investigating."

GOING THROUGH THE GARBAGE

They've made this rule for a lot of reasons—some health, some hygiene, but mostly just smell.

DISRESPECTING THE NUNS

Technically, Sister Lapis is a sister, not a nun, but she still shouldn't be disrespected.

Solution to Episode Four

the principal's office.

grabbed Jake, took the pencil from her, and marched her down to

"How dare you talk to me like that!" Sister Lapis said as she

"None of your business!" Jake replied.

"What are you doing out here?"

It was at that moment that Sister Lapis came out of the library.

Jake held the lucky pencil above her head and shouted, "Eureka!"

"It was wrapped in a used tissue,
and it was actually behind the trash can!"

HOW SERIOUS IS THAT CRIME?

**DEPENDS
ON HOW OFTEN
YOU DO IT**

For some crimes, it's like,
the first time is no biggie, but the
second time is concerning.

**NOT THAT
SERIOUS**

I mean, I guess you can be punished,
but usually it's not a big deal.

**VERY, VERY
SERIOUS**

This is not the kind of thing
you want to mess around with.

WHAT'S THE NORMAL PUNISHMENT FOR THAT?

SIT BY THE FENCE DURING RECESS

Jake doesn't mind this because there are always a couple of criminals to question on the fence.

AFTER-SCHOOL DETENTION

Getting held after school is a nightmare. But Jake can survive any nightmare.

POTENTIAL EXPULSION

Oh *no*! No more school? What ever would she do?

CLUES & EVIDENCE

Jake argued that going through the garbage wasn't a serious crime the first time. It depended how often you did it.

Sister Lapis pointed out that the punishment for crimes that were not that serious was after-school detention.

Principal Applegreen said that crimes that were very, very serious were not punished by sitting by the fence during recess.

Loitering in the hall was not punished by expulsion.

Sister Lapis insisted that Jake deserved to be expelled for her crime!

HINT

Sterling frequently had to sit by the fence for going through the garbage.

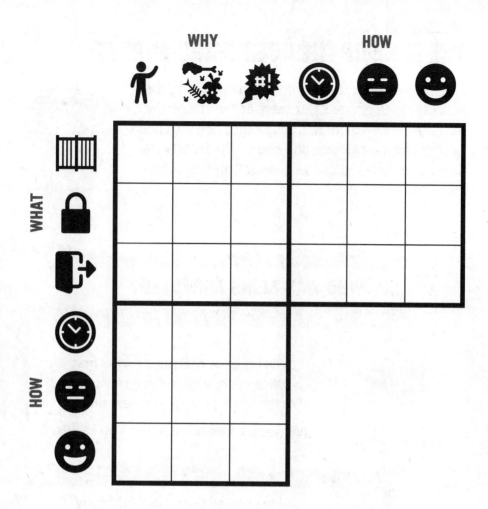

WHY

HOW

WHAT

HOW

_____

WHY?

_____

HOW?

_____

WHAT?

EPISODE SIX
THE CASE OF THE OVERHEARD ARREST

Jake was led back to class empty-handed. Sterling was sad. Brick gloated. But then, at the end of the day, the entire school was abuzz with news: Officer Copper was on campus, and one of the faculty was being arrested! The Sacred Kidney Cat Burglar had been caught!

WHO WAS BEING ARRESTED?

COACH RASPBERRY JR.

His team of mathletes wins first place every year. (If you're bad at math: First place is the best place.)

(6'1" • RIGHT-HANDED • BLUE EYES • BLOND HAIR)

PRINCIPAL APPLEGREEN

He's served the school faithfully for the last fifteen years, winning its coveted Best Principal Award for fourteen of them. (He launched a very unpopular calligraphy initiative that year.)

(5'11" • RIGHT-HANDED • BLUE EYES • BALD)

MRS. RUBY

She's a nice (and very stylish) teacher, definitely not an internationally infamous jewel thief. What would make you think that?

(5'6" • RIGHT-HANDED • GREEN EYES • RED HAIR)

Solution to Episode Five

"Jake was disrespecting the nuns, and it's very, very serious—potential expulsion!"

"Oh," said Principal Applegreen. "I don't think we need to expel her. We should all practice forgiveness, right?"

Jake and Sister Lapis both had a lot to say about that, and they talked over each other to do it.

Principal Applegreen sighed. "Fine. I'm confiscating this. Consider it a warning," and he took Sterling's lucky pencil. This made absolutely no one happy, but he seemed to think it was the end of the matter.

WHAT DID THEY HAVE ON THEM?

A BIG BUNCH OF CASH

In terms of things you can steal, this is one of the most universally tempting.

(MEDIUM-WEIGHT)

***THE* SACRED KIDNEY**

To Jake, it just looks like a rock. But apparently it's the petrified kidney of St. Sarcoline.

(HEAVYWEIGHT)

A LETTER

A stolen letter? Well, its value really depends on what it says....

(LIGHTWEIGHT)

WHERE HAD IT BEEN?

JANITORIAL CLOSET

He's got so many mops in there. Who needs this many mops? A janitor, I guess.

THE ONLY CAFETERIA IN THE SCHOOL

They have the best food of any cafeteria in the school.

THE CHAPEL

A great place to go once a week to be bored for an hour.

CLUES & EVIDENCE

Principal Applegreen has been waving around a letter he had found.

Mrs. Ruby was heard saying that she was in the cafeteria just for a bite to eat.

Of course, Jake knew that *the* Sacred Kidney was always kept in the chapel.

The Sacred Kidney had been stolen! Okay, that's a pretty big deal.

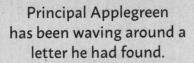

HINT

Mrs. Ruby had a medium-weight item. (And she claimed it belonged to her.)

THE CASE OF THE MISSING JAKE

Everyone thought the unmasking of the Sacred Kidney Cat Burglar was the wildest thing that was going to happen all day. But during the last hour of the school day, it was discovered that one of the students was missing: Jake! The school was closed and evacuated, and a search began: Where was she? No matter how many nuns, teachers, and volunteer tattletales the school recruited, they couldn't find her. Can you?

WHO ALL IS IN THE SCHOOL?

JAKE

She's the best detective at Sacred Kidney. She's probably the only detective at Sacred Kidney, too.

(4'2" • RIGHT-HANDED • GREEN EYES • BLOND HAIR)

PRINCIPAL APPLEGREEN

He was absolutely furious that he had to look for Jake just then.

(5'11" • RIGHT-HANDED • BLUE EYES • BALD)

SISTER LAPIS

She's got better things to do than this. For example, there's a sale at the local bedazzled habit store.

(5'2" • RIGHT-HANDED • BROWN EYES • BROWN HAIR)

OFFICER COPPER

Officer Copper was tired of being called to this church/elementary school.

(5'6" • RIGHT-HANDED • GREEN EYES • RED HAIR)

Solution to Episode Six

"It was Coach Raspberry Jr., who stole *the* Sacred Kidney from the chapel!"

"I found this letter in your office!" Principal Applegreen yelled at Coach Raspberry Jr. "It's a letter saying, 'I'll have the latest relic for you tonight! Meet me at the usual spot.' And it's signed 'Coach Raspberry'!"

"I don't need to sell any relics! This is ridiculous!"

But despite his denials, he was hauled away by Officer Copper, and all Jake could think was that something felt amiss.

WHERE ARE THEY CURRENTLY?

THE BOILER ROOM

The boiler makes a spooky knocking sound, and it smells weird. Also, everyone says it's haunted. People have seen things....

(INDOORS)

THE CHAPEL

Dark shadows lie spookily across already-pretty-spooky statues.

(INDOORS)

THE PRINCIPAL'S OFFICE

Locked up nice and tight to make sure that nobody gets in there while school is closed.

(INDOORS)

THE STEPS OUT FRONT

This is the only real way in or out of the school, except for all the ways Jake knows.

(OUTDOORS)

HOW DID THEY GET THERE?

TWO WORDS: *VENTILATION SYSTEM*

With access to a good ventilation system, there's almost nothing you can't do.

BEING SUPER STILL AND SILENT

This is one of the all-time best strategies for sneaking, no question.

NOT TRYING TO HIDE AT ALL

Sometimes not trying to hide is the best way to stay hidden.

WEARING A RIDICULOUS MUSTACHE

There's no better way to disguise yourself than wearing a ridiculous mustache.

CLUES & EVIDENCE

Principal Applegreen was searching the boiler room.

A note was found torn up in the trash:
Eht noitalitnev metsys saw ton sroodtuo.

The person in the chapel was being super still and silent.

Jake always said if she needed to sneak around the school, she would use two words: *ventilation system*.

Officer Copper was wearing a ridiculous mustache.

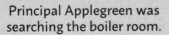

Where was Jake?

HINTS

The note with the clue on it was written with each word spelled backward.

WHO? _____

WHERE? _____

HOW? _____

THE END OF THE SCRIBBLED LINE

Was Jake right? Or was Principal Applegreen? The one and only thing they knew for sure is that just one of them was still going to be at Sacred Kidney tomorrow. That is, of course, unless one of the other two suspects was behind it after all.

WHO WAS IT?

BRICK

This kid is a punk bully, and nothing would make Jake happier than proving he deserved to be kicked out.

(4'7" • RIGHT-HANDED • BROWN EYES • BROWN HAIR)

PRINCIPAL APPLEGREEN

Jake's not sure if she hates him specifically or if she just hates all authority everywhere.

(5'11" • RIGHT-HANDED • BLUE EYES • BALD)

MISS SAFFRON

She's a nice teacher everybody seems to love. The perfect disguise.

(5'2" • LEFT-HANDED • HAZEL EYES • BLOND HAIR)

JAKE

Most kids couldn't break into the principal's office and get *him* expelled. But Jake's not most kids.

(4'2" • RIGHT-HANDED • GREEN EYES • BLOND HAIR)

WHAT IS THE CLUE THAT REVEALED EVERYTHING?

RASPBERRY'S LETTER

There's something weird about the signature here, or what it's signed with.

(LIGHTWEIGHT)

A BIG BUNCH OF CASH

The only thing that's more dangerous than a big bunch of cash is two big bunches of cash.

(MEDIUM-WEIGHT)

THE FERRET

If you look into this ferret's eyes, they will reveal all the secrets of the universe.

(MEDIUM-WEIGHT)

***THE* SACRED KIDNEY**

Why is this old, petrified body part even worth stealing?

(HEAVYWEIGHT)

WHY WERE THEY GETTING KICKED OUT?

RECKLESS DRIVING

It certainly wasn't wreckless driving.

VIOLATION OF ZONING LAWS

Some of the zoning laws are particularly strict.

GENERALLY BEING A BULLY

This isn't technically illegal, but it is highly frowned upon.

SELLING OFF THE SCHOOL'S RELICS

Sacred Kidney has a bunch of expensive relics...but fewer than it used to!

CLUES & EVIDENCE

Principal Applegreen would never drive recklessly. He values his car too much.

Brick has never even heard of zoning laws, nor is he able to violate them.

Miss Saffron had a big bunch of cash. She claimed she got it from Mrs. Ruby!

Jake was holding up a heavyweight clue.

The person who would be selling relics was holding Raspberry's letter.

The person who had the ferret was driving recklessly.

Miss Saffron was not bullying anyone.

It was Raspberry's letter that gave away the culprit!

HINT

Miss Saffron was a repeat offender of zoning-law violations.

WHY

WHAT

WHO?

WHAT?

WHY?

When all the heat had died down, Jake sat on the front steps of her school, chewing on the end of a piece of licorice. The janitor came up to her and congratulated her on a job well done.

"Thanks," Jake said. "But I was only doing what my client hired me to do."

"That's *exactly* what I'm congratulating you for," the janitor replied. Then he whipped off his mustache to reveal the familiar eyebrows (and the rest of the face) of Deductive Logico, Jake's detective hero!

"LOGICO!" she screamed, before remembering to act cool. "Are you ready to join the Detective Club?" Logico asked.

"It was Principal Applegreen selling off the school's relics, and Jake knew it from Raspberry's letter!"

"Ah! You see," Jake declared, "Principal Applegreen presented that letter as proof that Coach Raspberry intended to steal the Sacred Kidney. But look closely at Raspberry's signature!" Everybody did.

"You'll see the faint rainbow coloring of Sterling's lucky pencil! But *how* would Coach Raspberry have gotten Sterling's lucky pencil? I know that it has been here in the principal's office all day, not more than a few inches away from Principal Applegreen's hand!"

"So what are you saying?" Principal Applegreen scoffed.

"I'm saying you forged the letter and, at the last minute, decided it needed to have Coach Raspberry's signature. So you grabbed the nearest pencil to you, and it turned out to be Sterling's. So when you forged the incriminating document, you only incriminated yourself!"

"How could I have forged his signature?"

"How? You took a year off to take that calligraphy program, despite losing Principal of the Year because of it, and we all know how important that stupid award is to you. Give it up, Applegreen. You're busted!"

"Why I oughta!" he shouted, and lunged at Jake. But just when he was about to grab her, he was brought down cold by Sister Lapis, who had used *the Sacred Kidney* to knock him over the head. He fell to the ground, unconscious. Sister Lapis screamed, because *the Sacred Kidney* had cracked in two.

And then they saw what was inside it, and Jake said, "I think that's why Principal Applegreen was trying to frame Coach Raspberry for stealing it." Because what Sister Lapis was now holding in her hand was the largest emerald any of them had ever seen. It turns out the Sacred Kidney wasn't a kidney at all. It was really a giant gemstone with a chunk of rock around it. Quickly, the church stepped in to keep the relic safe. They locked it in a safe and buried it deep within an abbey, where nobody else could steal it.

EXHIBIT B:
THE CURRENT BEST MAP OF THE IMPOSSIBLE MAZE

JULIUS

IN

THE MYSTERY OF
THE UNIVERSE

JULIUS HAD BEEN LOOKING FORWARD TO THE WINTER HOLI-
day all year: He was going to visit his uncle Irratino and stay
at the Investigation Institute. This was a dream come true!

Julius never really fit in at school. In class, he was always
asking his teachers their least favorite question: "Why?"

But no matter how many times they answered, he could
always ask again. They would be excited to answer at first, then
they would be annoyed, then they would be frustrated, and

then, finally, they would be done with him. And still, Julius was not satisfied.

Surely, he believed, there must be some final reason for everything. There must be some explanation that would suffice, once and for all.

And that's what he was hoping for at the Investigation Institute: He wanted not to learn just anything, but to learn the ultimate answer to all the questions of life and living. This might seem like a pretty big request, but it was what his uncle Irratino said his institute was dedicated to solving.

"We investigate mysteries wherever they lead," Uncle Irratino had said, "and using whatever means necessary. Some people"—he said this with a smile—"think that only logic should be used to solve a mystery. But we disagree; we believe that logic can only get you so far. In order to use logic, you must first have insight! And insight is what we study."

The Investigation Institute had everything: crystal balls, marot cards, dowsing rods, pendulums, and more. Could these objects predict the future? Could they peel back the fabric of reality and reveal the true nature of existence, hiding just behind the veil? Could they allow us to understand not only the world that we live in, in its infinite mystery and complexity, but, in fact, ourselves? To all of these questions, Irratino answered simply, "We'll find out!"

But at this particular moment, as Julius rode in the back of the limo that Uncle Irratino had sent to pick him up, Julius wasn't wondering about the meaning of life and the true nature of the universe. He was wondering about a mystery that was so much smaller, and that yet, to him, seemed that much more important.

You see, someone had slipped Julius a note asking him to meet the first night he arrived at the Investigation Institute. But they hadn't signed the note, nor explained why they wanted to meet. And despite Julius knowing it was a bad idea to follow an anonymous note that asked you not to share its contents with anyone, he also knew that his curiosity was going to get the better of him.

After all, like his uncle Irratino had said, he would solve this mystery no matter where it led, and using any means necessary. Would he get to the bottom of it?

Again, in the words of Uncle Irratino: We'll find out!

This is *The Mystery of the Universe*.

EPISODE ONE
WHO SENT THE SECRET NOTE?

Julius was in the back seat of the car as it drove up to the Investigation Institute. He had a note slipped into his pocket that said, "MEET ME TONIGHT." He knew that the note was from someone who was at the Institute, but who? He could wait and find out when he arrived, but Julius typically found it was safer to speculate.

WHO WROTE THE NOTE?

UNCLE IRRATINO

Julius's uncle and the leader of the Investigation Institute.

(6'2" • LEFT-HANDED • GREEN EYES • BROWN HAIR)

NUMEROLOGIST NIGHT

They're the smartest person at the Institute, but that doesn't mean they're the best.

(5'9" • LEFT-HANDED • BLUE EYES • BROWN HAIR)

CORAL

She's the only other kid at the Institute. Unfortunately, Julius doesn't like her. He *loves* her.

(4'5" • RIGHT-HANDED • BLUE EYES • BROWN HAIR)

Detectives! The solution to each mystery will appear upside down at the beginning of the next one. Don't flip ahead until you think you know who did it!

WHERE WERE THEY?

THE IMPOSSIBLE HEDGE MAZE

Once, a man stumbled out of this maze after being lost in it for twenty years....

THE GRAND CHATEAU

There are more rooms in this chateau than Julius has seen in his life.

THE OBSERVATION TOWER

They built this to test some theories about gravity, but it also just has a great view.

Uncle Irratino was studying in his office, one of the many, many rooms of the Grand Chateau.

The smartest person at the Institute was not at the observation tower.

The note told Julius to meet at the impossible hedge maze—whoever would be there must have written it!

HINT

Since Uncle Irratino was in the Grand Chateau, and Numerologist Night was not at the observation tower, Coral must be at the observation tower!

WHO

UNCLE IRRATINO

NUMEROLOGIST
NIGHT

CORAL

WHERE

THE IMPOSSIBLE
HEDGE MAZE

THE GRAND CHATEAU

THE OBSERVATION
TOWER

WHO?

WHERE?

EPISODE TWO
WHERE IS NUMEROLOGIST NIGHT?

Julius crept inside the impossible hedge maze. He had been warned not to enter—by Uncle Irratino, by his parents, and by the sign out front—and yet, he knew he had to find Numerologist Night without getting lost among the hedges.

WHERE WAS NUMEROLOGIST NIGHT?

THE UPSIDE-DOWN FOUNTAIN

It seems like the water in this fountain flows up? It's perplexing, to say the least.

(WEIRD VIBES)

THE CENTER OF THE MAZE

This is the center of the maze. Legend has it that somebody once somehow found it.

(GREAT VIBES)

THE LONELY TOWER

A short squat tower that stands just high enough to let you see how complex this maze is.

(BAD VIBES)

Solution to Episode One

HOW DO YOU GET THERE?

TAKE ALL RIGHTS

This is a tried-and-true way to solve a lot of mazes.

TAKE ONLY LEFTS

If taking all rights solves some mazes, taking all lefts must solve some, too.

ALTERNATE TAKING LEFTS AND RIGHTS

This is how most people tend to solve mazes. But do most people know what they're doing?

If you wanted to get to the place with bad vibes, you had to alternate taking lefts and rights.

The upside-down fountain just wasn't right: The only way to get there was by taking all lefts.

Julius had a hunch that Numerologist Night would be at the center of the maze (and he listened to his hunches).

HINT

If you wanted to get to a place with great vibes, you had to take all rights.

WHERE

THE UPSIDE-DOWN FOUNTAIN

THE CENTER OF THE MAZE

THE LONELY TOWER

HOW

TAKE ALL RIGHTS

TAKE ONLY LEFTS

ALTERNATE TAKING LEFTS AND RIGHTS

WHERE?

HOW?

THE SECRET CASE OF THE SECRET

"The only way to solve Numerologist Night's murder,"
Irratino said, "is to figure out the secret they were
trying to reveal." Only Julius could aimlessly explore the
grand chateau without drawing attention. But there was
more than one secret hidden in these halls. Julius would
need to discover where each secret would be hidden
before he could figure out what their secret was.

WHAT'S THE SECRET?

A SMUGGLING OPERATION

The villain could be smuggling anything.
Like crystal wands or dowsing rods.

AN UNLICENSED ZOO

You can make a lot of money
with an unlicensed zoo. You can
also just have a good afternoon.

A PRIVATE LABORATORY

Why would someone need to
hide a laboratory in an institute
dedicated to investigating reality?

A LITERAL GOLD MINE

Like, not a moneymaker.
Someone might be secretly mining
gold beneath the building.

Solution to Episode Two

He found the center of the maze by taking all rights!

And sure, he found Numerologist Night, but he also found that they were dead. And standing over them was none other than Uncle Irratino. "Uncle!" Julius exclaimed.

Irratino turned to Julius. "Did you get a note, too? They wanted to share some big secret with us. But somebody wanted to stop them. We have to figure out who. I wish I could send you to a safe place, but nothing would reveal that you knew something more than you suddenly getting sent away. No, the only way to solve this problem is to solve this mystery."

WHERE IS THIS SECRET HIDDEN?

THE ATTIC

It's filled with cobwebs and boxes, and it always seems like twilight.

(BAD VIBES)

THE BALCONY

You can look over the grounds, and the woods around them, and feel really happy.

(GOOD VIBES)

THE PARLOR

A great place for entertaining guests, reading an old book, or just plain pondering.

(GOOD VIBES)

THE PRESIDENT'S OFFICE

This is Irratino's office, but that doesn't mean he was in there. He loves wandering off.

(GOOD VIBES)

A smuggling operation
would unquestionably be in
a place with bad vibes.

There's an old expression
at the Institute: "There's a literal
gold mine in the president's office."
Maybe it means something?

Julius received a note
written in code from his uncle
that read: *Anu nli cen sedz ooc
ou ldo nl yber unonth ebal con y.*

Julius had a hunch that the
big secret was in the parlor.

HINT

The note written in code just has the spaces between the
words rearranged. Maybe writing it out without spaces
will help!

WHAT

A SMUGGLING
OPERATION

AN UNLICENSED
ZOO

A PRIVATE
LABORATORY

A LITERAL
GOLD MINE

WHERE

THE ATTIC

THE BALCONY

THE PARLOR

THE
PRESIDENT'S
OFFICE

WHAT?

WHERE?

THE ROOM WITH FOUR SECRET PASSAGES

Julius knew there was a private laboratory somehow hidden in this room, accessible only by secret passage. But what he didn't know was that there were in fact several secret passages in this room, and they were all opened in different ways. He'd have to figure out how to open all of them to figure out how to find the right one.

WHICH SECRET PASSAGE LEADS TO THE SECRET LABORATORY?

THE BOOKSHELF

It rotates, but slowly, so that the books don't go flying.

(GOOD VIBES)

THE FIREPLACE

There's a small plaque that says the Institute is not responsible for injuries sustained while using this secret passage.

(WARM VIBES)

THE GRANDFATHER CLOCK

Ironically, this clock belonged to Uncle Irratino's grand*mother*.

(OLD VIBES)

A PORTRAIT

This is a portrait of Uncle Irratino's great-grandfather. He seems very stern.

(WEIRD VIBES)

Solution to Episode Three

"There's a private laboratory in the parlor!"

Julius knew that this was true more than he'd ever known anything. Somehow, in the parlor of the Grand Chateau, there was a hidden laboratory.

That didn't make any sense, but when he told Irratino about his deductions, Irratino told him, "You must go there and investigate! Only then will you know the truth!"

HOW DO YOU OPEN IT?

PULLING A CANDLESTICK FROM THE WALL

This is an all-time mystery classic. You know the Investigation Institute had to build one themselves.

A SMALL WOODEN BUTTON ON THE FLOOR

You could easily stub your toe on this.

TAKING A CERTAIN BOOK OFF THE SHELF

It's a how-to on astral projection. It says that it's easiest when you've been knocked out!

KNOCKING ON THE MANTEL

Classic, confident, cool. Knocking on the mantel is the best way to open a secret door.

An ancient legend said that
you could open a passage behind a
portrait by knocking on the mantel.

Julius knew you couldn't open a passage with
warm vibes by taking a book off the shelf.

A small wooden button on the floor opened
either the passage behind the grandfather
clock or the one behind the bookshelf.

Julius found scraps of paper,
which had been ripped up, that read
*ETH ERFNGTARHAD OKCLC SI TON
EEDPON THIW TEH EDOOWN TTONBU.*

**The secret passage that led to
the underground laboratory
was opened by pulling a
candlestick from the wall.**

HINT

When Julius unscrambled the scraps, they read, "The
grandfather clock is not opened with the wooden button."

WHICH

THE BOOKSHELF

THE FIREPLACE

THE GRANDFATHER CLOCK

A PORTRAIT

HOW

PULLING A CANDLESTICK FROM THE WALL

A SMALL WOODEN BUTTON ON THE FLOOR

TAKING A CERTAIN BOOK OFF THE SHELF

KNOCKING ON THE MANTEL

WHICH?

HOW?

EPISODE FIVE
THE SECRET OF THE SECRET LAB

Julius stumbled into the dark and spooky lab, but although he found it, he didn't find its operator. He knew he needed to figure out who was running this lab as fast as he could, before the person running it returned. To do that, he'd have to figure out what kind of lab it was, and what they were trying to research.

WHO IS RUNNING THE LAB?

ALCHEMIST RAVEN

She claims she can turn lead into gold, but only when nobody is watching.

(5'8" • RIGHT-HANDED • BROWN EYES • BROWN HAIR)

CRYPTOZOOLOGIST CLOUD

They love studying weird animals, like Bigfoot, or the Loch Ness monster, or a platypus.

(5'7" • RIGHT-HANDED • GRAY EYES • WHITE HAIR)

TECHNO-MAGUS MOSS

She has an unbelievable magick power: She can set up a printer...WITH HER MIND.

(5'4" • LEFT-HANDED • GREEN EYES • BROWN HAIR)

Solution to Episode Four

"The secret laboratory is behind the fireplace, and you access it by pulling a candlestick from the wall!"

And so that's what Julius did. He grabbed a candlestick and pulled it off the wall, and the flames in the fireplace began to flicker and die, and a small brick door slid open slowly behind them.

Julius stepped over the still-hot embers and snuck into the darkness. He crept his way through the passage, until he stumbled into the secret that he sought....

WHICH KIND OF LAB IS IT?

A COMPUTER LAB

Just because a computer is involved doesn't mean that magick can't be involved, too.

A POTIONS AND POISONS LAB

There's only one way to really tell if something is a potion or a poison: Drink it.

YOUR CLASSIC ALCHEMY LAB

Similar to a potions and poisons lab, except you're not supposed to drink anything here.

WHAT ARE THEY RESEARCHING?

IMMORTALITY

Living forever sounds really great, until you get stuck in a hole or something.

TOTAL KNOWLEDGE

What if you could know everything about anything? Would it be worth it?

WINNING THE LOTTERY

Years of occult research and not one psychic has done this. Hmm...

CLUES & EVIDENCE

Okay, first things first: Obviously Alchemist Raven would be running an alchemy lab.

The person who loved studying weird animals wanted to live forever, so they could study ones that hadn't even evolved yet.

No alchemist was interested in total knowledge; they were interested in the here and now.

Sure, you could use a poison to kill someone, but studying potions could grant immortality.

From all the computers, Julius suspected it was a computer lab.

You could use a computer to study total knowledge. That's what the internet is for, right?

HINT

WHO   WHICH

WHAT

WHICH

WHO?

WHICH?

WHAT?

THE GREATEST ESCAPE

Julius took off through the tunnels beneath the Investigation Institute, but he got lost almost immediately. They were more confusing than the hedge maze! But then, in the darkness, someone took his hand and led him to freedom. But who was it? Where did they lead Julius? And how did they find their way?

WHO HELPED JULIUS ESCAPE?

UNCLE IRRATINO

Honestly, he's a pretty swell uncle, so it could definitely have been him who saved the day, no question.

(6'2" • LEFT-HANDED • GREEN EYES • BROWN HAIR)

CORAL

If she showed up and saved the day, that would be, like, so incredibly cool.

(4'5" • RIGHT-HANDED • BLUE EYES • BROWN HAIR)

NUMEROLOGIST NIGHT

Sure, they're supposedly dead, but that doesn't mean their ghost can't help. Does it?

(5'9" • LEFT-HANDED • BLUE EYES • BROWN HAIR)

Solution to Episode Five

"It was Techno-Magus Moss, in a computer lab, studying total knowledge!"

Just as Julius said those words, another hidden door to the computer lab flew open, and Julius saw the silhouette of Techno-Magus Moss. Quickly, he hid between two servers. But when she flicked on the lights, Julius could see just how many computers were working, and how they were all pumping some kind of energy into a small ruby.

He could also see that he needed to run! So he did.

WHERE WOULD THEY LEAD JULIUS?

EVEN DEEPER INTO THE TUNNELS

You know that old saying: The best way out is through...an unfathomably terrifying darkness.

THE GRAND CHATEAU BASEMENT

There's a whole bunch of old books down there, and some new T-shirts.

THE DEEP DARK WOODS

The forest surrounds the Grand Chateau in all directions. Deeply dark...but only at night. In the day, they're the bright, nice woods.

HOW WOULD THEY FIND THEIR WAY?

A REALLY GOOD MEMORY

You can memorize anything if you're willing to take the time to do it.

A PHONE

Having a phone is like having a crystal ball, a dowsing rod, and a spell book put together.

A MAP AND COMPASS

You also need a light to be able to see these. A major downside.

CLUES & EVIDENCE

If it was the ghost of Numerologist Night, they would have led Julius even deeper into the tunnels...never to escape!

Nobody who had been to the deep dark woods would go there again, so nobody could lead Julius there by memory.

Coral never used a phone! She was strictly analog. So cool.

The tallest suspect still used their really good memory to get around the Institute.

Whoever it was led Julius into the deep dark woods!

HINT

The ghost of Numerologist Night would have had to use a phone to get through these tunnels. Even dead people need navigation aids.

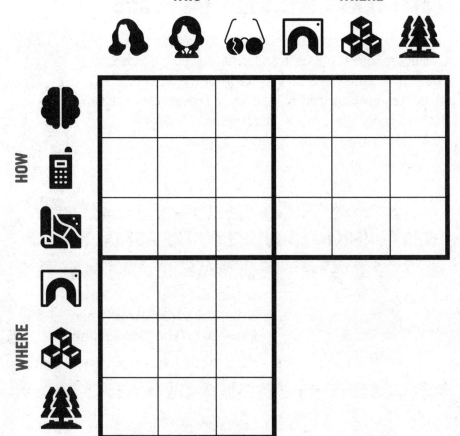

WHO

WHERE

HOW

WHERE

WHO? _____

WHERE? _____

HOW? _____

EPISODE SEVEN
A MYSTERY ON THE ASTRAL PLANE

Julius was knocked unconscious, and he either had a vivid dream as his neurons and synapses shook loose or, alternatively, he had a mystic vision of the astral plane, where he found himself able to fly wherever he wanted. But he wasn't alone in the astral plane: Someone was going to confront Julius.

WHO CONFRONTED JULIUS ON THE ASTRAL PLANE?

CORAL

Somehow, she's even cooler when she's manifesting her presence on the astral plane.

(4'5" • RIGHT-HANDED • BLUE EYES • BROWN HAIR)

TECHNO-MAGUS MOSS

She's astral projecting with the help of a VR rig she has set up in the Institute.

(5'4" • LEFT-HANDED • GREEN EYES • BROWN HAIR)

THE ENTITY

It has some strange, uncanny pulsating force behind it, like a creature that's a dream.

(INFINITE • ALL-HANDED • ONE EMPTY EYE • NO HAIR)

NUMEROLOGIST NIGHT

They're back from the dead, which meant very little to them, because numbers never die.

(5'9" • LEFT-HANDED • BLUE EYES • BROWN HAIR)

Solution to Episode Six

It was Coral, and she led him into the deep dark woods using only a map and compass!

"This is so cool! Wait, where are we going?" Julius asked.

"This is the only way," Coral said. "I already know what will happen."

But suddenly Julius had a not-too-pleasant idea. What if Coral wasn't rescuing him? What if Coral was taking him to the woods so that there'd be no witnesses when whatever was about to happen happened?

Suddenly, he felt something on the back of his neck, and he passed out.

WHERE WOULD THEY BE?

A BIG PUFFY CLOUD

Nothing feels more like astral projection than running across a big puffy cloud.

THE COSMIC VOID

It's nothing. But it's so much nothing that it's really something.

A MOUNTAINTOP

It's so serene and peaceful, especially since you don't have to actually climb up there.

THE HAPPY MEADOW

It's a beautiful peaceful meadow where nobody is ever murdered.

WHAT WEAPON WOULD THEY USE?

A DREAM SWORD — Like a regular sword, but made of dreams.

A LANCE OF EMOTION — This is like one of those big poles that jousters carry...when they're furious!

NEGATIVE THOUGHTS — Normally, it's fine to have these, but on the astral plane, they can kill!

INFINITE CHAOS — That's right. Not just a little chaos. Big chaos. Huge chaos! Infinite chaos!

CLUES & EVIDENCE

Even though it was a happy meadow, there would still be negative thoughts there.

A creature known only as the Entity would be floating in the cosmic void.

The suspect on the big puffy cloud would be using a dream sword.

Techno-Magus Moss would not wield the dream sword.

Coral would have a furious jouster's weapon.

The true enemy was using infinite chaos on Julius!

HINT

Numerologist Night would particularly enjoy his dream sword.

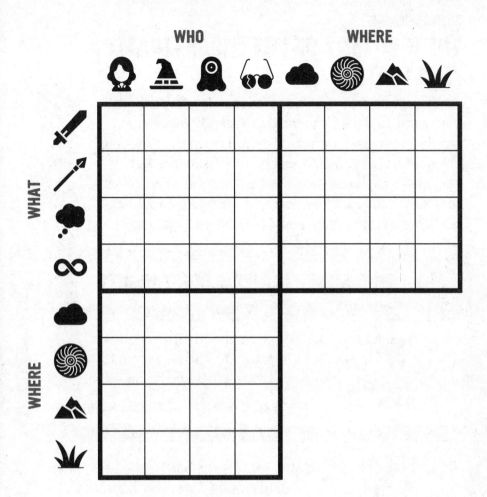

WHO?

WHERE?

WHAT?

EPISODE EIGHT
THE MYSTERY OF THE INVESTIGATION INSTITUTE

Julius woke up in the morning woods and walked back to the Institute. There, he found that Techno-Magus Moss had died. Overnight, the ruby had overloaded and exploded, killing her and destroying most of her computers. But when Julius explained everything to his uncle, Irratino was confused. "Moss wasn't on campus when Night was killed." Someone else must have killed Numerologist Night!

WHO KILLED NUMEROLOGIST NIGHT?

DR. SEASHELL, D.D.S.

He's the Institute's private dentist. He also has some far-out theories about the universe.

(5'7" • RIGHT-HANDED • GREEN EYES • GRAY HAIR)

CORAL

Is she good? Is she bad? Is she somewhere in between? Does she like Julius?

(4'5" • RIGHT-HANDED • BLUE EYES • BROWN HAIR)

NUMEROLOGIST NIGHT

They were up and walking around again. This is a weird kind of ghost that can talk and touch stuff.

(5'9" • LEFT-HANDED • BLUE EYES • BROWN HAIR)

UNCLE IRRATINO

Out of an abundance of caution, Irratino insisted he also be included in the list of suspects.

(6'2" • LEFT-HANDED • GREEN EYES • BROWN HAIR)

WHERE ARE THEY HIDING OUT NOW?

THE IMPOSSIBLE HEDGE MAZE

Once, a man stumbled out of this maze after being lost in it for twenty years...so Julius was lucky he had made it out the first time!

THE GRAND CHATEAU

Julius has explored the chateau for days, and there are still dozens of rooms he has never seen.

THE OBSERVATION TOWER

One of the downsides of hiding in a tower is that people can see the tower for miles.

THE GREAT GATES

Okay, so, maybe *great* is doing them too much of a favor. They're good gates, alright?

WHY ARE THEY HELPING MOSS?

TO STOP THE END OF THE WORLD

What would you do to stop the end of the world? A lot? A little? Something in between?

TO MAKE A WHOLE HEAP OF MONEY

You can make so much money helping someone make a lot of money.

BECAUSE THEY WERE SO, SO BORED

You'd be surprised what people will do if they're bored. Like, solving puzzle books, even.

THEY ARE ACTUALLY SIBLINGS

Whoa! Twist!

CLUES & EVIDENCE

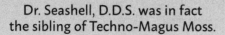

Dr. Seashell, D.D.S. was in fact the sibling of Techno-Magus Moss.

Coral always liked to spend time in the observation tower.

The person at the great gates would not kill someone just because they were so, so bored.

The person in the impossible maze wanted to make a whole heap of money.

Uncle Irratino was so, so bored.

The person who killed Night wanted to stop the end of the world.

HINT

Numerologist Night wanted to make a whole heap of money.

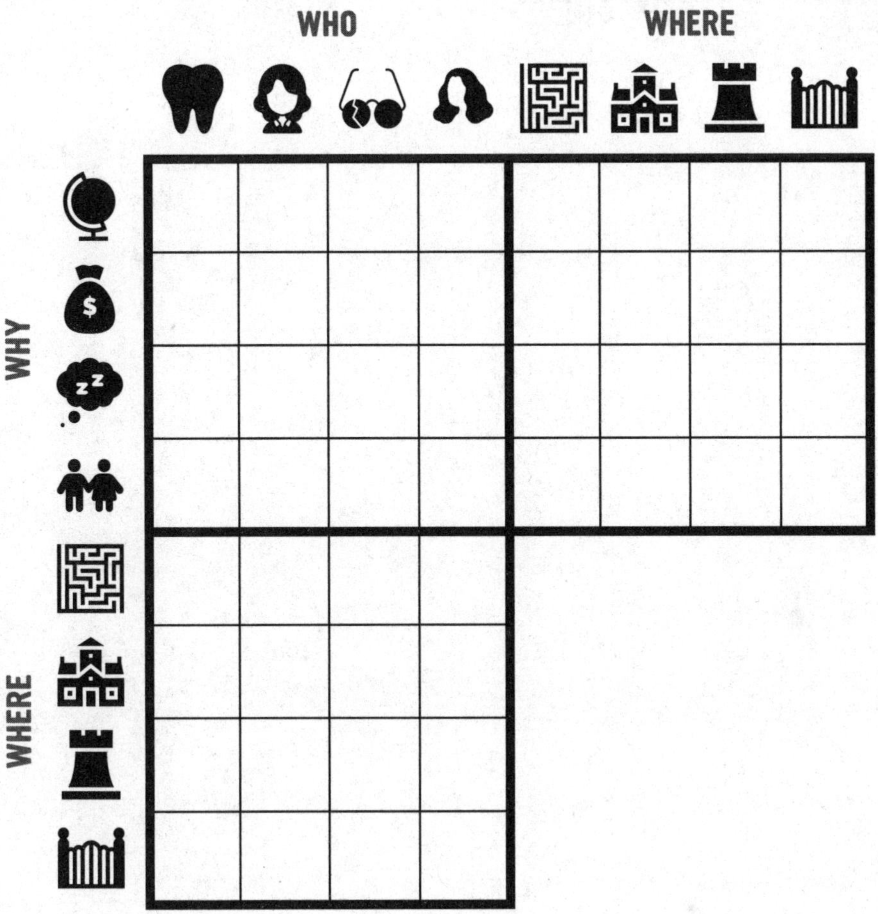

WHY

WHERE

WHO?

WHERE?

WHY?

"Excuse me, you two," said a voice. Julius turned toward it and saw a man he had never met before, but whose eyebrows immediately impressed him. "I'd like to offer you an invitation," the stranger said, as he passed an envelope to Julius.

"Oh, yeah. I saw this in the ruby projection, too," Coral said. "Hi, Logico."

"Hello, Coral," Logico replied. "You haven't been replying to my letters."

"That's because I'm not interested in joining your Detective Club. I already have all the mysteries I need here at the Institute. But I know that Julius is interested. I've already seen him accept."

"It was Coral, in the observation tower, to stop the end of the world!"

Julius couldn't believe it. "Coral, you're a murderer?!"

"No! Numerologist Night is fine! But yes, I did put him to sleep with a mixture of Tired-Eyes Tea and...other things. But he should be waking up about now!"

Julius sensed that Coral was telling the truth. But he still had his constant question: "Why?"

Coral explained, "One week ago, I was up in the observation tower, observing things with my telescope, when I saw Techno-Magus Moss sneaking around in the deep dark woods. So I followed her through the tunnels, and I found her secret lab. There, I watched through my telescope as she completed her machine to grant her total knowledge. When she flipped the switch, the computer-charged crystals showed every possible future, and in each of them, this knowledge brought a terrifying creature into our reality."

"The Entity," Julius replied.

"There were a million different futures that Techno-Magus Moss and I glimpsed that night. Some bad, some worse. All of them ended the same way, with the Entity destroying the world. But for one, which offered a way to stop it. If I knocked Numerologist Night unconscious, I could motivate Iratino to ask you to investigate it, which would set the events into motion for you to confront the Entity on the astral plane. You were the only one who I knew wouldn't be tempted by having all your questions answered."

"But I love asking questions."

"Exactly. You love asking questions too much to ever stop! If you had all the answers, what would you do with yourself? So thanks for saving the day. I'm just sorry I had to knock you out to send you to the astral plane."

"What? You knocked me out?"

"Yes, Julius! Ugh, it's so hard talking with people who haven't had a glimpse of all possible futures."

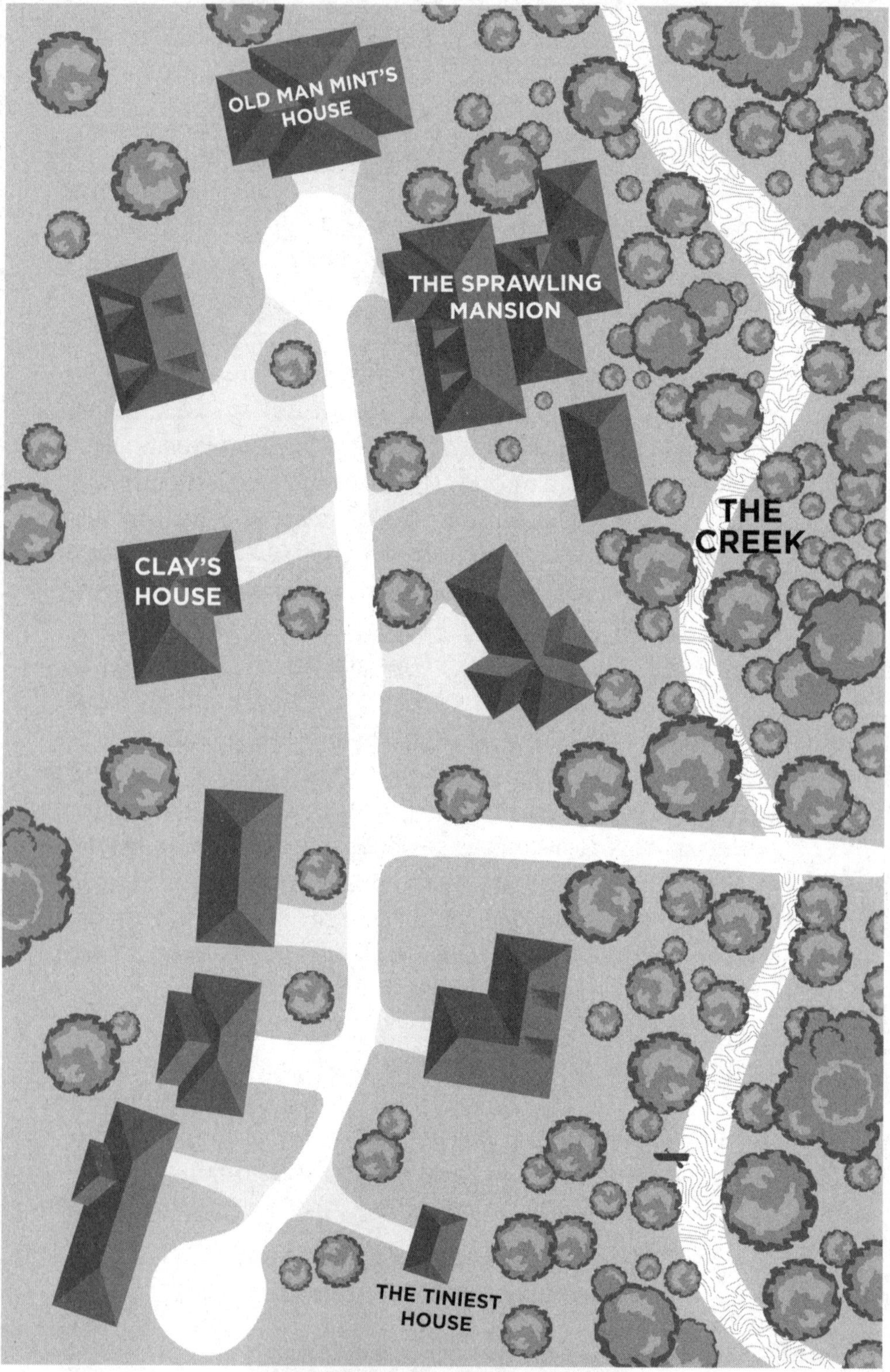

OLD MAN MINT'S HOUSE

THE SPRAWLING MANSION

THE CREEK

CLAY'S HOUSE

THE TINIEST HOUSE

EXHIBIT C:
A MAP OF CLAY'S NEIGHBORHOOD

BUSTER McPAWS

IN

THE CRIME OF THE CENTURY

THE NEIGHBORHOOD WAS DIFFERENT AT NIGHT. ANYBODY who roamed these streets knew that. No kids selling lemonade or moms mowing lawns. The streets were empty, dark, and dangerous.

But that was just how Buster McPaws liked it.

His pet human, Clay, didn't know this, but Buster was the top cat detective in the world. And that was a tough category, too. Much better than the top dog detective, Buster thought. In fact, the top dog detective probably wasn't that much better than the worst cat detective. And so, every night, when Clay and the other humans were asleep, Buster would leave the comfort of Clay's house and patrol the neighborhood from one end of the street to the other. Maybe that wild raccoon was trying to dig through the trash again. Or maybe there was something going on at Old Man Mint's spooky old house. Whatever it was, he'd see it.

Buster McPaws knew these streets like the back of his, well, paws, and he was determined that crime was not going to rule this neighborhood. Not while he was around. And soon, criminals would quake in fear of the name...*Buster McPaws!*

But tonight was different. Tonight, even Buster was afraid. He had seen some horrible crimes before, but nothing he had ever seen was as bad as this. When Buster got back to his garage, ready to sneak in through the cat door and snuggle up to his Clay, he discovered the most terrible crime scene he had ever had the misfortune to discover.

Someone had stolen his food. A few loose kibbles were scattered across the cement floor of the garage, all that was left of his nightly feast.

And they'd stolen not just his food, but his dish, as well. Someone had taken everything that Buster McPaws cared about, and they had done it with no remorse or regret.

Only the evilest of criminals would do such a thing. So it would take the bravest of detectives to stop them.

No matter how afraid he might have been, Buster knew that someone had to clean up these streets. Someone had to rid the neighborhood of this terrible menace. Someone had to get back his dinner. And that someone was going to be him.

Buster McPaws was going to hit the streets. He was going to stick his nose where it didn't belong. He was going to dig his way to the bottom of this crime. He was going to scratch the surface of Clay's neighborhood and uncover the terrible criminal underground beneath it.

Tonight, Buster McPaws was going to solve *The Crime of the Century*.

OPERATION: FUR-ENSICS!

Buster investigated the scene of the terrible crime. Not one square inch of that garage went unsniffed— including a particularly suspicious rake. He knew only three suspects who could have done such a thing. And they each would have done it differently.

WHO STOLE THE TREATS?

ROMEO RACCOON

A smooth operator who lives off the neighborhood trash. He's already wearing a mask!

(2'1" • RIGHT-PAWED • YELLOW EYES • BROWN FUR)

OLD MAN MINT

He lives in the spooky old house at the end of the street. And face it: That's suspicious.

(6'2" • RIGHT-HANDED • GREEN EYES • BALD)

CLAY

Sometimes the worst betrayals come from the ones you love the most. Could Clay really do such a thing?

(4'11" • LEFT-HANDED • BROWN EYES • BLACK HAIR)

Detectives! The solution to each mystery will appear upside down at the beginning of the next one. Don't flip ahead until you think you know who did it!

HOW WOULD THEY DO IT?

GOING THROUGH THE CAT DOOR

This is the only way in or out of the garage.

A GARAGE DOOR OPENER

This is the typical way non-cats get into a garage. It seems to work by magick.

USING THE RAKE AS A GRABBY THING

Yes, Buster thought. *This rake could be used as a grabby thing....*

CLUES & EVIDENCE

The mask-wearing smooth operator was the only one who could fit through the cat door.

Buster smelled the rake, and he was certain it wasn't Clay who used it.

Whoever stole the treats definitely used the rake as a grabby thing!

HINT

Since Romeo Raccoon would have gone through the cat door, and Clay didn't use the rake, Clay must have used the garage door opener.

WHO

ROMEO RACCOON

OLD MAN MINT

CLAY

HOW

GOING THROUGH THE CAT DOOR

A GARAGE DOOR OPENER

USING THE RAKE AS A GRABBY THING

WHO?

HOW?

EPISODE TWO
THE CAT BURGLAR STRIKES!

Buster had heard of people calling themselves cat burglars, but nothing could compare to the real thing. Before Buster could confront Old Man Mint, he had to sneak into his spooky old house. There were at least three ways inside, and a specific way to get into each of them. Buster was going to carefully analyze his options before he made his attempt.

WHERE WOULD HE GET IN?

THE FRONT DOOR

This is probably how Old Man Mint expects Buster to enter.

(GROUND FLOOR)

THE CHIMNEY

Up too high for a human to use. But nothing is impossible for a cat.

(TOP FLOOR)

THE BASEMENT WINDOW

It's cracked open just a teeny-tiny bit.

(GROUND FLOOR)

Solution to Episode One

"It was Old Man Mint, using the rake as a grabby thing!"

Buster didn't realize that he was living in the same neighborhood as a monster. But the facts didn't lie, and logic was on his side. So he snuck down the streets and made it to Old Man Mint's spooky old house.

Lightning cracked. Thunder roared.

And Buster went to confront the beast that lived inside.

HOW WOULD HE DO THAT?

CLIMBING A TREE

Buster didn't like to climb trees. But that didn't mean he couldn't.

SQUEEZE MODE

All cats have the ability to shrink themselves through tiny spaces; this is called squeeze mode.

SECRET DISGUISE

Buster could dress up as a dog, or a package. Or even a different cat.

CLUES & EVIDENCE

If Buster wanted to go in
how Old Man Mint expected,
he would have to mix it up
by using a secret disguise.

Buster would not need
to use squeeze mode to
get in from the top floor.

After considering all
the options, Buster knew he
would need to use squeeze
mode to get inside.

If Buster wanted to get in through the chimney, he would
have to climb a tree.

104 · MURDLE JR.

WHERE

THE FRONT DOOR

THE CHIMNEY

THE BASEMENT WINDOW

HOW

CLIMBING A TREE

SQUEEZE MODE

SECRET DISGUISE

WHERE?

HOW?

SNEAKING THROUGH THE MANSION

Buster snuck through the spooky old mansion, making careful note of who was there and using his talents of being completely silent, extra alert, and very small. Sure, in a lot of situations, he didn't like being a soft little cutie pie. But sometimes it came in handy. Tonight, he would use it to track down his mortal enemy.

WHO WAS IN THE HOUSE?

MRS. RUBY

An infamous jewel thief whose name is ironic, because it's usually the other person who misses their ruby.

(5'6" • RIGHT-HANDED • GREEN EYES • RED HAIR)

BUDDY THE DOG

If you asked Buster, Buddy was tied with all other dogs for the title of worst dog.

(3'2" [LONG] • AMBIDOGTROUS • BROWN EYES • BROWN FUR)

OLD MAN MINT

In his head, Buster calls him the beast. Because only a beast would be so horrible as to steal Buster's food.

(6'2" • RIGHT-HANDED • GREEN EYES • BALD)

AN UNKNOWN FOURTH PERSON

Buster didn't know who the heck this was. They smelled different than anything he had ever smelled.

(?'?" • ?????-HANDED • ????? EYES • ????? HAIR)

Solution to Episode Two

"Buster McPaws climbed in through the basement window using squeeze mode!"

When Buster landed on the basement floor, he quickly hid. He was in the lair of the beast. Now the hard part began. Now he had to prove that he deserved to call himself the world's greatest cat detective.

WHERE WERE THEY?

THE BASEMENT

It's filled with cardboard boxes. But Buster didn't have time to sit in them.

THE GRAND ENTRANCE

This was directly above where Buster was at that moment.

THE COURTYARD

This is like an indoor room that's actually outdoors. It's a courtyard!

THE LOCKED UPSTAIRS ROOM

This was the only locked room in the whole mansion.

CLUES & EVIDENCE

Buddy the Dog could be heard barking in the indoor/outdoor room.

Buster saw Mrs. Ruby in the room filled with cardboard boxes.

A fourth, unknown person could be smelled from behind a locked door.

Where was the beast?

HINT

The beast was Old Man Mint, of course. And he definitely wasn't in the basement.

WHO

MRS. RUBY

BUDDY THE DOG

OLD MAN MINT

AN UNKNOWN
FOURTH PERSON

WHERE

THE BASEMENT

THE GRAND
ENTRANCE

THE
COURTYARD

THE LOCKED
UPSTAIRS
ROOM

_____

WHO?

_____

WHERE?

THE MYSTERY BEHIND THE LOCKED DOOR

Buster was probably not the world's bravest detective. There were a few things that terrified him: garbage trucks, fireworks, and whatever horrible monster was behind that locked door, pounding in a rage. He would have to figure out who was behind the locked door, and why these people had them locked up.

WHAT'S BEHIND THE LOCKED DOOR?

ANOTHER CAT

I'm not saying Buster is lonely, but he was hoping that this was who was behind the door.

(2'3" [LONG] • LEFT-PAWED • GREEN EYES • BLACK & WHITE FUR)

A TRAINED ORANGUTAN

When you're making a list of the possibilities behind a door, you have to consider all of them.

(4'6" • RIGHT-HANDED • BROWN EYES • RED FUR)

THE PRESIDENT OF DRAKONIA

This seems pretty far-fetched. But do you know what else is far-fetched? A cat detective.

(5'10" • RIGHT-HANDED • GRAY EYES • WHITE HAIR)

AN EVIL MURDERER

Maybe the other three people in the house aren't the bad guys. Maybe they've got the bad guy locked behind this door.

(7'2" • RIGHT-HANDED • FLAMING RED EYES • WILD BLACK HAIR)

Solution to Episode Three

responded by pounding on the door—this time in a rage.

small hole in the locked door. And whoever was on the other side

horror...that Old Man Mint was slipping *Buster's kibbles* through a

to slink after him all the way up the stairs until he saw...with

he had a tail himself, so he was always practicing. And he managed

because easy was which him, tailed he found him, Buster when And

"It was Old Man Mint, in the grand entrance!"

WHERE DID THEY COME FROM?

KIDNAPPED FROM THE CIRCUS

Usually, it's more common for the circus to do the kidnapping, no?

A CARDBOARD BOX WITH CHEESE UNDER IT

The one downside to this plan is that somebody else has to pull the string connected to the stick.

FOUND IN THE CREEK

If so, it would fall under creek rules: finders, keepers.

BROKEN OUT OF JAIL

Did they break a real criminal out of jail only to put them in another, less-secure jail?

No cat would fall for the old cardboard-box-with-cheese-under-it trick.

The President of Drakonia was not even at the circus, much less kidnapped from it.

If it was an evil murderer, then they broke him out of jail.

A left-pawed victim was not kidnapped from the circus.

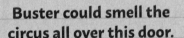

Buster could smell the circus all over this door.

HINT

Embarrassingly enough, it was the President of Drakonia who fell for the old cardboard-box-with-cheese-under-it trick. (If word of that got out, it would surely cost her votes!)

WHAT

ANOTHER CAT

A TRAINED ORANGUTAN

THE PRESIDENT OF DRAKONIA

AN EVIL MURDERER

WHERE

KIDNAPPED FROM THE CIRCUS

A CARDBOARD BOX WITH CHEESE UNDER IT

FOUND IN THE CREEK

BROKEN OUT OF JAIL

_____

WHAT?

_____

WHERE?

EPISODE FIVE
THE CASE OF THE CIRCUS CAGE

Orangutan Orange had never liked his life in the circus. He didn't enjoy performing, especially considering his performance required him to juggle flaming chainsaws. But one day, he was kidnapped, and he liked being kidnapped even less.

WHO KIDNAPPED ORANGUTAN ORANGE?

OLD MAN MINT

If anybody asked him, he said he was just visiting the circus and enjoying some time with his grandchildren. A likely story!

(6'2" • RIGHT-HANDED • GREEN EYES • BALD)

MRS. RUBY

Mrs. Ruby once stole the *Mona Lisa*. She's stolen three submarines. She can definitely steal an ape.

(5'6" • RIGHT-HANDED • GREEN EYES • RED HAIR)

KID KHAKI

This is the most serious kid you've ever met. His favorite hobby is accounting, and his greatest ambition is to grow up.

(4'1" • RIGHT-HANDED • BROWN EYES • BROWN HAIR)

Solution to Episode Four

"It was a trained orangutan, and it was kidnapped from the circus!"

When Buster snuck into the locked room, he discovered that—far from being a raging monster—the trained orangutan was locally famous!

He was Orangutan Orange, a circus performer who did a routine in which he juggled flaming chainsaws.

Using the language that all animals understand, Orangutan Orange told Buster the story of how he came to be there....

WHERE WOULD THEY DO IT?

THE BIG TOP

Honestly, the size of this tent is more impressive than the rest of the circus.

THE HALL OF MIRRORS

According to a plaque, this hall of mirrors was used in a famous old movie nobody remembers.

THE CAGES

The cages are cramped and the animals are sad. But the circus makes money!

HOW WOULD THEY DO IT?

A GIANT CRANE

You could use a giant crane to steal an ape, but then the question is: How do you get the crane?

THE MAGIC DISAPPEARING ASSISTANT TRICK

An old magic trick where the magician puts an assistant in a tank and they disappear, but in this case, instead of an assistant, it's an ape.

YOUR CLASSIC GETAWAY VAN

"I don't know why you're overcomplicating this. Just throw the ape in the van and go."

CLUES & EVIDENCE

Kid Khaki was under the big top, mildly entertained by the show.

Old Man Mint would use a classic getaway van. That's how they used to do things in his day.

You couldn't use a giant crane at the big top: too much tent in the way!

Mrs. Ruby was not in the hall of mirrors.

Orangutan Orange was locked in the cages when he was kidnapped.

A big crane was used to steal the ape, much to the amazement of the onlookers, who thought it was part of the show.

HINTS

WHO?

WHERE?

HOW?

THE CASE OF THE COMPROMISED WITNESS

Clay burst out of the mansion and ran through his neighborhood, going as fast as he could. Someone caught up to Clay and captured him. But who? And where? And how did they do it?

WHO CAUGHT CLAY?

MRS. RUBY

Getting Mrs. Ruby to knock out a witness for you would be a real steal.

(5'6" • RIGHT-HANDED • GREEN EYES • RED HAIR)

OLD MAN MINT

He just wanted to steal an ape, and now he's chasing a neighborhood kid.

(6'2" • RIGHT-HANDED • GREEN EYES • BALD)

MAIL CARRIER MARZIPAN

They're the new mail carrier, and they raise an impressive eyebrow at these shenanigans.

(6'0" • RIGHT-HANDED • BROWN EYES • BLACK HAIR)

Solution to Episode Five

The following text appears upside-down:

"It was Mrs. Ruby, in the cages, with a giant crane."

Just as Orangutan Orange finished telling the story, Old Man Mint and Mrs. Ruby returned. Buster hid just in time.

"Has anyone seen my cat?" Clay asked, stepping into the room.

"Hey, is that the orangutan that was stolen from the circus?" The looks on Mrs. Ruby's and Old Man Mint's faces told him the answer. They also told him that he needed to run.

He did, and they chased after him.

WHERE DID THEY CATCH HIM?

THE STREET

Clay's been to many neighborhood block parties on this street. But maybe he's attended his last party.

(OUTDOORS)

THE CREEK

Once, Clay and Buster went exploring in this creek, and they found a bunch of cool rocks.

(OUTDOORS)

CLAY'S HOUSE

Clay's house had never looked so appealing to him. So close, and yet so far!

(INDOORS)

HOW DID THEY DO IT?

A BIG BAG

The perfect way to get rid of a nosy neighbor is to put 'em in a big bag.

THE OL' ONE-TWO

A classic boxing combination. First you hit 'em with one punch, and then, in a shocking twist, you hit them with another punch.

TIRED-EYES TEA

Get him to drink a glass of this brand-name beverage and he'll be napping in no time.

CLUES & EVIDENCE

The person with Tired-Eyes Tea had green eyes that were wide awake.

Mrs. Ruby had been taking boxing lessons (after all, she takes everything else) and was the only one who could do the ol' one-two.

The mail carrier was delivering mail to a place that was indoors.

The person in the street did not have a box of Tired-Eyes Tea.

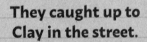

They caught up to Clay in the street.

HINTS

The mail carrier would never have let the bag out of their hands. Also, there was something weird about this mail carrier. Something not exactly professional. Something curious...

WHO   WHERE

WHO?

WHERE?

HOW?

THE CASE OF THE RESCUED PET HUMAN

Buster was not going to be able to rescue his owner/servant from the literal bind he had gotten himself into. But that didn't mean he wasn't going to try. But just when Buster thought that all was lost, suddenly, someone joined the fray alongside him, and together, they were able to free Clay. Who was it?

WHO HELPED BUSTER McPAWS RESCUE CLAY?

BUDDY THE DOG

Buster wonders if Buddy will defy the entire history of dogs and do something useful for a change.

(3'2" [LONG] • AMBIDOGTROUS • BROWN EYES • BROWN FUR)

MAIL CARRIER MARZIPAN

They claim to just be delivering the mail. But something is suspicious about Marzipan.

(6'0" • RIGHT-HANDED • BROWN EYES • BLACK HAIR)

ORANGUTAN ORANGE

He could have made his escape. Why would he come back to help Clay?

(4'6" • RIGHT-HANDED • BROWN EYES • RED FUR)

ROMEO RACCOON

A smooth operator who lives off the neighborhood trash. He's already wearing a mask!

(2'1" • RIGHT-PAWED • YELLOW EYES • BROWN FUR)

Solution to Episode Six

Clay gulped. How was he going to get out of this one?

    The next thing he knew, he was tied to a chair in the basement of Old Man Mint's home. Things weren't looking good for the apenappers, either: Orangutan Orange had gotten away in the confusion. "You made us lose our ape!" Old Man Mint said. "Now we're going to make you pay."

Fortunately, Clay had also taken boxing lessons, so he evaded her punches. So instead, she grabbed him.

"It was Mrs. Ruby, in the street, with the ol' one-two!"

HOW DID THEY HELP?

TERRIFYING THE KIDNAPPERS

It's hard to terrify kidnappers because, for one, they're not afraid of kidnapping.

ONE WORD: EXPLOSIVES

Not sure exactly how this would help, but it would definitely be exciting.

LIGHTNING-FAST REFLEXES

They never lose that game where you try to slap the back of the other person's hands.

SLOBBERING OVER EVERYTHING

Buster thinks this is the grossest way you can possibly accomplish any goal.

WHY DID THEY HELP?

TO SLEEP EASY AT NIGHT
Sometimes you have to repay a favor if you want to sleep easy at night.

SOME KIND OF EVIL PLAN
Just because someone's doing something good doesn't mean they're doing it for good reasons.

THE MAIL MUST NOT BE STOPPED
Do you hear me? The! Mail! Must! Not! Be! Stopped!

MERCENARY WORK IS ALWAYS WELL PAID
Sometimes you work for a scared kid, sometimes for a multinational arms dealer. Either way!

CLUES & EVIDENCE

Buster was sure that Buddy the Dog would rescue Clay only if it was part of some kind of evil plan.

The ambidogtrous suspect would try to slobber over everything.

Mail Carrier Marzipan was determined that the mail must not be stopped.

The potential ally who might be motivated by the fact that mercenary work is always well paid had lightning-fast reflexes.

The tallest suspect could help with one word: *explosives*.

Romeo Raccoon did not feel like he owed Clay. He didn't feel like he owed anybody.

The villains were absolutely terrified by this new ally!

HINT

Buster had to admit that Romeo Raccoon had lightning-fast reflexes (and was much better than a dog).

WHO

HOW

WHY

HOW

WHO?

HOW?

WHY?

THE CASE OF THE NEIGHBORLY CRIMINAL

One of the people in the neighborhood had intended to buy the orangutan. But now that everything has fallen apart, they were probably going to try to remain in hiding. But Buster will not let this would-be purchaser of a stolen orangutan run free. They will pay for what they tried to buy!

WHO WAS PAYING FOR THE WHOLE OPERATION?

MAIL CARRIER MARZIPAN

They deliver all the mail. So they know where everybody lives. That's too much knowledge.

(6'0" • RIGHT-HANDED • BROWN EYES • BLACK HAIR)

CLAY

Sure, he seems like a good, respectable boy. But he could be hiding something terrible!

(4'11" • LEFT-HANDED • BROWN EYES • BLACK HAIR)

SIGNOR EMERALD

He's a jeweler of great renown, known for how fast he can make (and lose) a fortune.

(5'8" • LEFT-HANDED • BROWN EYES • BLACK HAIR)

EARL GREY

Yes, that's right, *that* Earl Grey. The tea magnate.

(5'9" • RIGHT-HANDED • BROWN EYES • WHITE HAIR)

Solution to Episode Seven

WHERE DO THEY LIVE?

THE GIANT SPRAWLING MANSION

Unlike Old Man Mint's place, this one has been kept up. It also has a pool.

(INDOORS)

THE TINIEST HOUSE ON THE STREET

The neighbors all complain about it, but they secretly love it, because it makes them feel good about their own houses.

(INDOORS)

CLAY'S HOUSE

Hmm. Whoever could it possibly be who lives here?

(INDOORS)

A CREEK BOAT

Have you ever heard of a house boat? Well, this one is on a creek!

(OUTDOORS)

WHY?

TO STEAL THE WORLD'S LARGEST EMERALD

It's a huge emerald that's technically owned by the church. But who really "owns" anything?

TO PUT HIS ACT IN A RIVAL CIRCUS

Circus-on-circus sabotage happens all the time. It's a competitive industry.

TO PROTECT THE POPULACE

A giant orangutan could be pretty dangerous to the local community.

TO KEEP HIM AS A PET

Look, everybody wants an orangutan as a pet. That's why it's illegal.

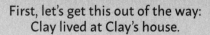

CLUES & EVIDENCE

First, let's get this out of the way: Clay lived at Clay's house.

Signor Emerald did not care about protecting the populace, like, at all.

Earl Grey, rich as he was, wanted to be richer. He wanted the world's largest emerald.

Mail Carrier Marzipan did not live in the giant sprawling mansion.

The person who wanted the ape to perform in a rival circus lived in the tiniest house on the street.

The person who lived on the creek boat just wanted to protect the populace.

The only person who could afford this trained ape lived in the giant sprawling mansion.

Based on Buster's experience, Clay would have wanted to keep the ape as a pet.

HINT

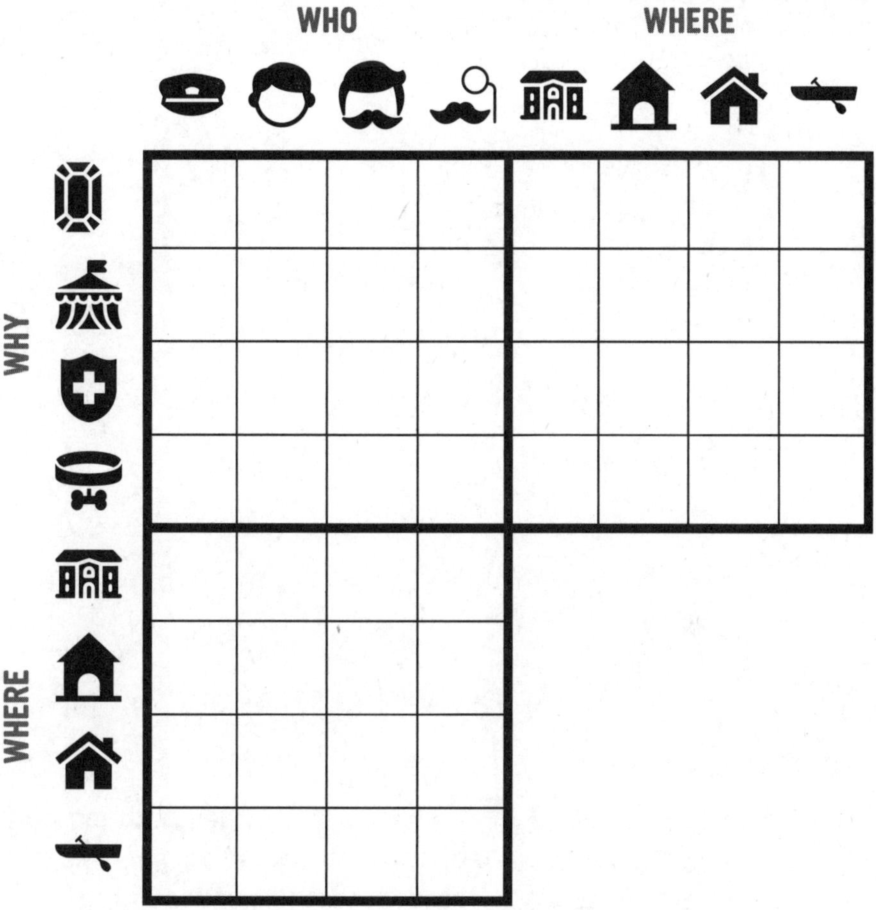

WHY

WHERE

_____

WHO?

_____

WHERE?

_____

WHY?

an ape, and saved the day! The police say I brought down the whole crime ring! I'm a hero! The greatest kid detective on the street! And who knows, maybe even in the whole world?!"

Buster didn't like this, but before he could passive-aggressively ignore Clay over it, Mail Carrier Marzipan walked up to both of them and whipped off their mail carrier hat, revealing a fedora underneath: The mail carrier was really Deductive Logico!

He handed Clay an envelope. Clay ripped it open and found an invitation to join the Detective Club. Clay read it and was overjoyed.

"Wow! Golly gee! Now I'm a real-life detective! I'd love to join, Mr. Logico. I'd love to become a junior detective and travel the world solving mysteries with the top crime-solvers of my generation!"

"It's not for you," Logico replied. "It's for your cat. Buster McPaws, you are hereby invited to join the Detective Club as our first cat member."

"It was Earl Grey, in the giant sprawling mansion, to steal the world's largest emerald!"

"Fine! I wanted the world's largest emerald, and so when I heard about that church that found the world's largest emerald inside one of their schools, I knew I needed to steal it. But it's hard to steal an emerald. Too much security. But you know what's easier to steal? A trained orangutan! Trained orangutans have almost no security! But with a trained orangutan, you can easily steal an emerald. They can climb walls, break down doors, and intimidate witnesses, and no one can trace it back to you!"

Buster McPaws never understood why the villains loved to explain their plans when they were caught. But Clay had another problem. He didn't understand why anybody would ever do anything wrong.

"Well, you shouldn't steal things!" Clay said. Buster knew it had nothing to do with "should," though. The world was a tough place, but we had to live in it. Buster McPaws didn't care about what happened to these criminals. Nor did he care about whatever lesson Clay was going to teach them about doing good. No, what Buster McPaws cared about was his food and his dish, and he had gotten them both back. And while Clay waited for the police to show up, he took them back to the garage.

But when he got to the top of Clay's driveway, he saw Orangutan Orange standing at the edge of the woods, staring back at Buster. Buster sat upright and looked at the orangutan, and the orangutan raised a hand to his head and saluted Buster. And then he vanished into the trees.

Buster McPaws wondered if he should be at all worried that there was a thieving orangutan running loose in the neighborhood. But ultimately, he decided that it was none of his business what this escaped ape wanted to do with his life. McPaws had his dish back. He had food to eat. He was happy.

Later, Clay came home, proud of how he had solved a mystery, going on and on about what a great detective he was. "And then she tried to punch me, but I dodged the punches! And I rescued

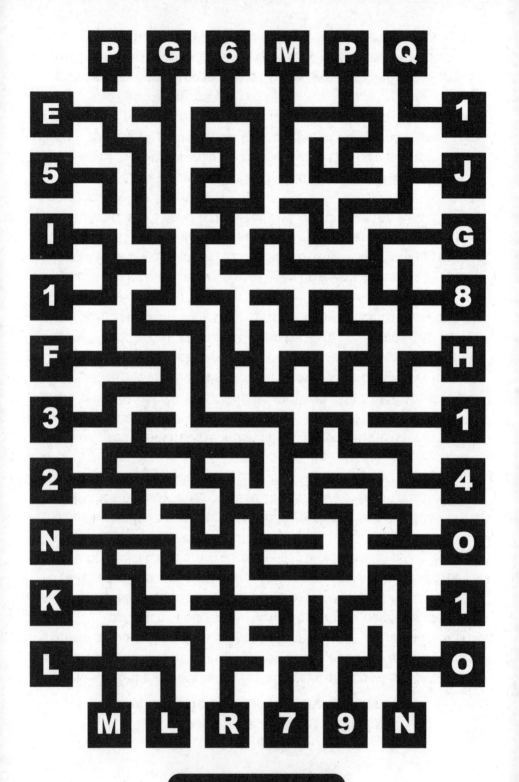

EXHIBIT D:
A HIGH-TECH CIRCUIT BOARD

OLIVIA

IN

THE CASE OF THE CORRUPT COMPUTER

EVERY DAY AFTER SCHOOL, OLIVIA WOULD HEAD DOWN TO her father's company, where she would help everyone with her favorite activity in the entire world: debugging software.

Now, some people might say that debugging software is boring, but to Olivia, it was paradise. Poring over thousands of lines of code looking for a single typo? Racking your brain to understand the complex logic of a dozen different subroutines? Examining a million lines of a spreadsheet to find the one cell that was mislabeled? These were Olivia's ideas, not just of a good time, but of the best time you could possibly have. What's not to like?

At first, her father tried to discourage her from spending all her free time working as a volunteer for his company. For one, it was bad for morale, as the professional programmers he had hired never enjoyed being outdone by a kid. Two, he thought his daughter should be out in the world, having new experiences, growing as a person, and enjoying her life, rather than hunched over a computer screen.

However, when his accountant showed him how much money Olivia was saving the company, he quickly changed his mind. Now she had her own workstation, and her own desk, too, which was also bad for morale, but her father didn't mind: If people were mad that a kid was better at computers than they were, then maybe that would encourage them to work harder.

One day, Olivia logged on to her machine and found that the company network was down. When she asked around, she discovered that nobody else could log on, either. And when she asked what people were doing about it, they told her, "Waiting for you to fix it."

Well, she was here now, and she was going to solve the problem. No matter how many lines of code she'd have to pore over.

No matter how many subroutines she'd have to unravel. No matter how many spreadsheets she'd need to study.

But when she looked into the issue a little closer, she realized that it wasn't an ordinary computer bug—no mere typo, this problem. This time, it was something a lot worse: A computer virus had managed to infect the company network.

And it was up to Olivia to stop it.

But little did Olivia know that fixing this computer virus was not going to be the end of the company's problems. In fact, it was only the beginning.

This is *The Case of the Corrupt Computer*.

EPISODE ONE
OLIVIA VERSUS THE VIRUS

Olivia knew that the first step to stopping the virus was to figure out what kind of virus it was. But she knew that to figure out what kind of virus it was, first she would have to discover what kind of file it had infected.

WHAT KIND OF VIRUS WAS IT?

SKULLBUG

You get this from picking up a strange USB drive or clicking on a weird link.

(VERY DANGEROUS)

MAXIMO 2000

This is a virus from back when the year 2000 was considered the future.

(NOT THAT DANGEROUS)

S.P.Y.WARE

Made by the nefarious organization S.P.Y., this software can track everything about you.

(NOT DANGEROUS BUT ANNOYING)

WHICH FILE TYPE HAD IT INFECTED?

VIDEOS

The user claimed the infected files were training videos, but really, they were all clips of cute cats.

DOCUMENTS

Like research papers and slideshows and copy edits of puzzle books in progress.

SETTINGS

These files store all your preferences, like mouse sensitivity and how loud you want the bass.

Skullbug only infects the
settings on your computers.

S.P.Y.Ware is known
to infect video files.

Olivia discovered that
the virus had definitely
infected a document file.

HINT

Since Skullbug infects the settings, and S.P.Y.Ware infects
videos, there's only one option left for Maximo 2000.....

WHAT

SKULLBUG

MAXIMO 2000

S.P.Y.WARE

WHICH

VIDEOS

DOCUMENTS

SETTINGS

WHAT?

WHICH?

EPISODE TWO
THE CASE OF THE TECHNO TRAITOR

Olivia put together a list of the top suspects at the company. Only three people had the computer knowledge needed to install the virus. To discover whodunit, she would need to figure out which department they worked in.

WHO UPLOADED THE VIRUS?

VICE PRESIDENT MAUVE

She's the go-to person for the toughest jobs—but has she started to resent it?

(5'8" • RIGHT-HANDED • BROWN EYES • BLACK HAIR)

EXECUTIVE EGGPLANT

As an executive, he's taken an oath to protect the company. Would an executive really lie?

(5'5" • LEFT-HANDED • GREEN EYES • BLACK HAIR)

THE GENIUS JERK JUNIPER

Sometimes adults tolerate a jerk who's good at their job. But they always regret it!

(5'2" • LEFT-HANDED • BLUE EYES • BROWN HAIR)

Solution to Episode One

"It was Maximo 2000, in the documents!"

Olivia smiled for the first time that day when she deleted Maximo 2000 from the system, cleaning the hard drives and restoring the full functionality of the company computers. Now, though, she had a new problem: No virus from the last millennium should be able to beat company security...unless it had help.
Someone at the company had installed this virus on purpose.

WHERE DO THEY WORK?

OFFICE MANAGEMENT

This is the only department that is absolutely needed, so (of course) it's the least respected.

METAVERSE DEVELOPMENT

This department is supposed to be developing a virtual world people can live inside. What it's really doing is wasting money.

CUSTOMER SERVICE

Olivia's father keeps saying they should cut this one: "If they're still customers, they don't need any additional service!"

The suspect who worked in office management had a last name that began with a letter connected to the 4 in the circuit board diagram. (See Exhibit D, at the beginning of this section.)

The jerk was assigned to customer service so that they and the customers could annoy one another.

Olivia was convinced that only someone who worked in the metaverse department would have the technical skill needed to commit the crime.

HINT

If Executive Eggplant worked in the office management department, and Juniper worked in customer service, then which one is left for Vice President Mauve?

**VICE PRESIDENT
MAUVE**

**EXECUTIVE
EGGPLANT**

**THE GENIUS
JERK JUNIPER**

WHERE

**OFFICE
MANAGEMENT**

**METAVERSE
DEVELOPMENT**

CUSTOMER SERVICE

WHO?

WHERE?

EPISODE THREE
THE CASE OF THE UNDEAD VP

When Olivia untied VP Mauve, she thought she might know what had happened to her. But all she knew was that she'd been hit on the back of the head with a heavy object. What hit her, and who was holding it? Each person would have used a different method, but only one of them actually did it!

WHO ATTACKED MAUVE?

VICE PRESIDENT MAUVE

Okay, so, it's unclear exactly how she would have tied herself up and knocked herself out, but we can't rule it out.

(5'8" • RIGHT-HANDED • BROWN EYES • BLACK HAIR)

THE IT GUY

The first thing you notice about this IT guy is his magnificent eyebrows.

(6'0" • RIGHT-HANDED • BROWN EYES • BLACK HAIR)

HAZEL

She's the daughter of one of the meanest executives, and the family resemblance is strong.

(4'3" • LEFT-HANDED • HAZEL EYES • BROWN HAIR)

THE BIG BOSS

He's also Olivia's dad, which he calls his second most important job.

(5'11" • RIGHT-HANDED • GREEN EYES • BROWN HAIR)

"It was Vice President Mauve, in metaverse development!"

Olivia used the network to search for Vice President Mauve, but she couldn't find her anywhere. So she went up to her office to see if there were any clues. And she sure found a clue: Mauve was tied up behind her desk!

WHAT DID THEY USE?

A RED STAPLER

No office would be complete without this classic office supply/deadly weapon.

A WHOLE BUNCH OF OLD CDs

Back in the Before Times, music was stored on these strange spinning discs....

A ROBOT CAT

Different from a regular cat in two major ways: It's a little less friendly, and it has laser eyes.

UNARMED

One of the worst weapons to use to attack someone is no weapon at all.

CLUES & EVIDENCE

The IT guy did not have a classic office supply on him.

The mean daughter wouldn't be caught dead with a bunch of old CDs.

If you didn't count the ropes, Vice President Mauve was unarmed. (And she was also unarmed if you *do* count them, because she didn't have the use of her arms.)

A black hair was found in between two old-timey discs.

The second-tallest suspect did not have a weapon with laser eyes.

A robot cat had been used to commit the crime!

HINT

Based on an office-supply inventory, Hazel definitely did not have a stapler.

WHO

VICE PRESIDENT MAUVE

THE IT GUY

HAZEL

THE BIG BOSS

WHAT

A RED STAPLER

A WHOLE BUNCH OF OLD CDs

A ROBOT CAT

UNARMED

WHO?

WHAT?

EPISODE FOUR
THE MYSTERY OF THE MISSING KID

When Olivia finally got the lights back on, Hazel was gone. But that couldn't be the end of the story. Olivia was determined to track Hazel down and make her pay for what she did (cost the company money). But first, she'd have to figure out how she fled!

WHERE DID HAZEL GO?

DRAKONIA

It's hard to say which is scarier: the haunted forests or the constant wars.

(COUNTRY)

NEW AEGIS

This is a great vacation spot, especially if you like sand.

(TOWN)

A NICE ENGLISH VILLAGE

It's just a regular peaceful English village: old houses, beautiful hills, and so, so many murders.

(TOWN)

THE S.P.Y. SATELLITE

The company has a minor investment in an orbital S.P.Y. satellite. No big deal; don't worry about it.

(GEOSYNCHRONOUS SPACE STATION)

Solution to Episode Three

"It was Hazel, with a robot cat!"

"You think that just because your dad is the CEO you're better than me?" Hazel asked.

"No!" Olivia replied. "I think I'm better than you because I'm not attacking people and installing viruses!"

"I think I'm better than you because I'm going to get away with it!"

Hazel pulled up an app on her phone and pressed a button, and all the lights in the office went off, casting them into darkness.

HOW DID SHE GET THERE?

A PREARRANGED STRETCH LIMO

Probably the classiest getaway vehicle you can request on your phone.

A PROTOTYPE TELEPORTATION MACHINE

So far, in testing, it's more of a disintegration machine.

A JETPACK

Probably the coolest means of travel, so long as you fix that pesky "horrible burns" issue.

A REALLY LONG SECRET TUNNEL

If you dug it with a shovel it would take about a thousand years. So, maybe use two shovels.

One thing Olivia knew about really long secret tunnels is that they absolutely never got you all the way to Drakonia.

You couldn't get to New Aegis in a prearranged stretch limo: They have a very strict rule against gas-guzzling vehicles.

The prototype teleportation machine is the only way you could get to the S.P.Y. satellite.

Olivia found a helpful clue written in the Next Letter Code: *RDBQDS STMMDK CNDR MNS KDZC SN MDV ZDFHR.*

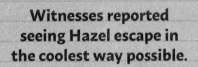

Witnesses reported seeing Hazel escape in the coolest way possible.

HINT

You can crack the Next Letter Code by replacing each letter with the next one.

WHERE

 DRAKONIA

 NEW AEGIS

 A NICE ENGLISH VILLAGE

 THE S.P.Y. SATELLITE

HOW

 A PREARRANGED STRETCH LIMO

 A PROTOTYPE TELEPORTATION MACHINE

 A JETPACK

 A REALLY LONG SECRET TUNNEL

WHERE?

HOW?

A DEADLY EXECUTIVE DECISION

Olivia and three of her fellow employees took off in the company jet to New Aegis. Unbeknownst to all of them, there was an accomplice aboard the jet. And when the plane was in the air, this accomplice attacked the pilot and hid somewhere on the plane.

WHO IS THE ACCOMPLICE?

EXECUTIVE EGGPLANT

He's paid more than a thousand of the lowest-level employees combined. But to be fair, the lowest-level employees are paid very little.

(5'5" • LEFT-HANDED • GREEN EYES • BLACK HAIR)

EXECUTIVE ASSISTANT OLIVE

One day, with a lot of hard work, she hopes to be an Assistant Executive.

(5'6" • RIGHT-HANDED • GREEN EYES • BROWN HAIR)

EXECUTIVE PRODUCER STEEL

She's going to head up production on the company's new streaming service.

(5'6" • RIGHT-HANDED • GRAY EYES • WHITE HAIR)

Solution to Episode Four

"Hazel fled to New Aegis with a jetpack!"

Olivia quickly calculated the top speed of a jetpack, and the top speed of the company jet, and she knew that she and her coworkers could arrive in New Aegis hours before Hazel. Then, when they finally caught up with her, Olivia could give her what she deserved: a lecture.

WHAT ARE THEY ARMED WITH?

THEIR WITS

If you're in a fight with someone and they're armed only with their wits, you're in luck!

(ZERO WEIGHT)

A BAZOOKA

Firing a bazooka in a plane is like detonating a stink bomb in an elevator: not good.

(HEAVYWEIGHT)

A PARACHUTE

How is this a weapon? Well, for one, there's a hole in it. Two, you could hit someone with it.

(MEDIUM-WEIGHT)

WHERE DID THEY DO IT?

THE WING

It would be really hard to murder somebody on the wing. But it would also be easy.

(OUTDOORS)

THE PASSENGER CABIN

They have a pool. Yes, that's right, a pool on a plane.

(INDOORS)

THE COCKPIT

This is definitely the most dangerous place to commit a murder...for the other passengers!

(INDOORS)

CLUES & EVIDENCE

A medium-weight weapon was indoors.

Executive Producer Steel was trying to take a phone call on the wing.

The shortest suspect was armed only with their wits.

A parachute was not in the passenger cabin (sorry, passengers).

The pilot was attacked while he was goofing off in the cockpit.

HINT

A helpful piece of career advice: Always be kind to the assistants; they're the only ones who ever pack a parachute.

WHO

WHAT

WHERE

WHAT

WHO?

WHAT?

WHERE?

EPISODE SIX
THE CASE OF THE CRASHING PLANE

"Error!" intoned a robotic voice throughout the plane. "The plane is going down!" Olivia calculated that she had about two minutes to figure out what was wrong with the plane and fix it before it crashed into that mountain she saw ahead. Was that enough time?

WHAT PART OF THE PLANE WAS SABOTAGED?

THE NAVIGATION SOFTWARE

The most perilous thing you could do would be to reverse up and down.

AUTOMATIC SEAT EJECTOR

Every seat could be rigged with an ejector. Hey, it could happen!

THE BATHROOM

You don't even want to know how a bathroom could be sabotaged.

Solution to Episode Five

"It was Executive Assistant Olivia, with a parachute, in the cockpit!"

"Yeah, okay!" Olive said. "Fine, I did it for Hazel. When she takes over, I'll get promoted!" Then she kicked the door open on the side of the plane and leapt out.

"Wait!" cried Olivia, because she had noticed the hole in the parachute. But it was too late. And the last thing they heard was Executive Assistant Olive shouting, "Nooooooooooo," as she fell.

HOW COULD SHE FIX IT?

BY TIGHTENING SOME BOLTS

You'd be surprised at how often just tightening some bolts can fix an issue.

DEBUGGING THE CODE

Olivia has debugged so much code she calls herself The Exterminator.

SHE CAN'T

Bad news, everybody!

WHICH TOOL WOULD SHE USE?

A MINI SAFETY WRENCH OLIVIA ALWAYS CARRIES

Lefty loosie and righty tightie, right? Or is it lefty less loose, righty right-off?

A FLASH DRIVE

It holds a bunch of software, and also a bunch of Olivia's favorite songs.

AN IN-FLIGHT MAGAZINE

It's not exactly clear how this would fix the jet, but there is a nice crossword inside.

CLUES & EVIDENCE

How could Olivia use an in-flight magazine to fix the jet? She couldn't.

If an automatic seat ejector had been sabotaged, she'd have to tighten some bolts.

There's no possible way she could use a safety wrench to debug code.

She couldn't fix the navigation software with an in-flight magazine.

Olivia had to use a flash drive to fix the plane!

HINT

The in-flight magazine was in the bathroom, where it was most needed.

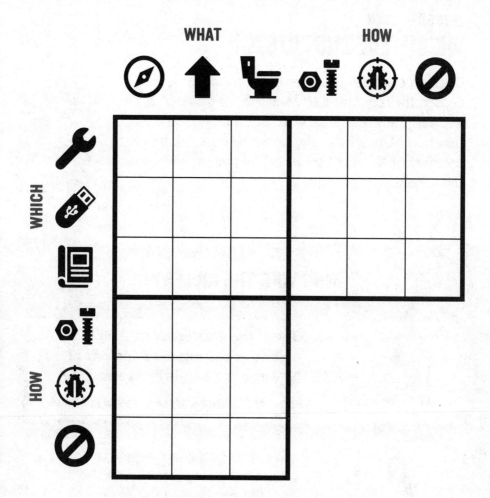

WHAT?
_____

HOW?
_____

WHICH?
_____

EXECUTIVE INDECISION

Once they had safely landed in the middle of the desert, they could see Mt. Aegis in the distance. It was definitely too far to walk. But what choice did they have? Unfortunately, along the walk, the last member of the flight crew was murdered. Who was it this time?

WHO WAS THE KILLER?

EXECUTIVE EGGPLANT

One of the greatest executives in the world at cutting costs and one of the worst at treating his workers well.

(5'5" • LEFT-HANDED • GREEN EYES • BLACK HAIR)

EXECUTIVE PRODUCER STEEL

She's going to struggle to get her next promotion if she dies out here in the desert.

(5'6" • RIGHT-HANDED • GRAY EYES • WHITE HAIR)

EXECUTIVE ASSISTANT OLIVE

She survived the fall, but she couldn't figure out where to go, and she has just been wandering in the sand.

(5'6" • RIGHT-HANDED • GREEN EYES • BROWN HAIR)

A DESERT HERMIT

He likes living in the desert, okay? It's clean. There's plenty of sand and sun. It's like the beach, but without fish.

(6'3" • RIGHT-HANDED • GRAY EYES • WHITE HAIR)

Solution to Episode Six

It was the navigation software, and Olivia debugged the code using a flash drive!

She did it just in time, too. Not in time to stop the jet from crashing, but definitely in time to prevent the plane from smashing into Mt. Aegis and killing them all. Instead, she guided it down to the sand dunes for a landing that completely destroyed the plane but miraculously kept everyone (else) alive.

WHAT WEAPON DID THEY USE?

A BAG OF SAND

There's a lot of sand around here, but not that many bags.

(HEAVYWEIGHT)

A GLASS DAGGER

Lightning struck the sand and turned it into this awesome dagger.

(LIGHTWEIGHT)

ANOTHER IN-FLIGHT MAGAZINE

This one contains an article about a bunch of thefts from a church school.

(LIGHTWEIGHT)

A BRIEFCASE FULL OF CASH

Honestly, why kill someone with this when you could just run away with it?

(MEDIUM-WEIGHT)

WHERE WAS THE CRIME COMMITTED?

THE BIG CACTUS

Okay, so it's not, like, mansion big. But for a cactus, it's pretty big.

(OUTDOORS)

THE JAGGED ROCK

A great landmark to help you find your way in the desert, or to murder someone beside.

(OUTDOORS)

THE WRECKED JET

It's the broken wreckage of a billion-dollar aircraft.

(INDOORS [SORT OF?])

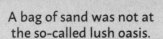

THE LUSH OASIS

Upon closer inspection, this is actually a mirage.

(OUTDOORS)

CLUES & EVIDENCE

A bag of sand was not at the so-called lush oasis.

The in-flight magazine was indoors (sort of?).

The head of production at the company's new streaming service had a lightweight weapon.

The person standing in a lush oasis had a name that began with the letter connected to the 2 in the circuit board diagram. (See Exhibit D, at the beginning of this section.)

A glass dagger was stuck into the big cactus.

Executive Eggplant had a glass dagger.

The murder took place at the jagged rock!

HINT

Since Executive Producer Steel had a lightweight weapon, you know she didn't have a bag of sand or a briefcase. To help you out further, she didn't have a glass dagger, either.

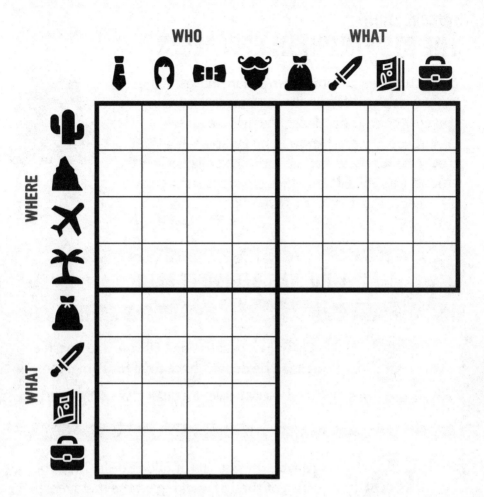

WHO?

WHAT?

WHERE?

THE BIG FINISH IN NEW AEGIS

Olivia stumbled into the town square in New Aegis, half conscious. "Virus," she mumbled. "Mauve tied up. Accomplice. Hazel, my rival. Jet travel. Executives. Desert. I know...one person behind it all... they're here in New Aegis." Then she collapsed on the ground. Can you put together the clues and figure out whodunit before she's revived?

WHO WAS BEHIND IT ALL?

THE BIG BOSS

Okay, just because he's Olivia's dad doesn't mean he doesn't have time for crime, too.

(5'11" • RIGHT-HANDED • GREEN EYES • BROWN HAIR)

VICE PRESIDENT MAUVE

Maybe she got sick of taking orders. Maybe she got tired of working on the metaverse.

(5'8" • RIGHT-HANDED • BROWN EYES • BLACK HAIR)

HAZEL

Obviously, Hazel was a key element of the scheme. But was she in charge of it?

(4'3" • LEFT-HANDED • HAZEL EYES • BROWN HAIR)

EXECUTIVE EGGPLANT

Did he have what it took to organize a conspiracy to overthrow the company's board?

(5'5" • LEFT-HANDED • GREEN EYES • BLACK HAIR)

Solution to Episode Seven

"It was a desert hermit, with a bag of sand, at the jagged rock!"

"Fine! I did it! You want to know why? Because I used to work for this company, before I got laid off, and then I had to move out to the desert."

"Surely," Olivia said, "you could have lived someplace better."

"Not cheaper!" the hermit exclaimed. Olivia would have tried to detain him, but he kept swinging his bag of sand, and the executives made an executive decision to flee.

WHERE WERE THEY HIDING?

MT. AEGIS

Could you hollow this out and build a secret laboratory inside it? Maybe!

(OUTDOORS)

THE SONIC OSCILLATOR

A giant dome that people claim can heal any injury, or at least just help you think.

(INDOORS)

THE UFO CRASH SITE

There's some debate as to whether the UFO is legitimate, but there's none as to whether it's profitable as a tourist attraction.

(OUTDOORS)

THE KITSCHY RESTAURANT

It has desert-themed desserts, which is confusing for everybody to spell.

(INDOORS)

WHAT WAS THEIR GOAL?

JUST A CONSEQUENCE OF COST CUTTING

Sometimes if you cut costs too much, you risk everything falling apart.

TO GET A PROMOTION

Killing several people is a great way to earn the respect of your superior officers.

TO GET A BETTER JOB SOMEWHERE ELSE

Murdering a bunch of people is a great way to get out of your current contract.

GETTING REVENGE ON OLIVIA SPECIFICALLY

Olivia has made a lot of enemies by being smart and awesome.

CLUES & EVIDENCE

A suspect with black hair wanted a better job somewhere else.

Executive Eggplant was not hiding at the Sonic Oscillator. Too loud!

Hazel did not now (and never would) care about cost cutting.

The person who wanted to get a promotion was hiding indoors.

The shortest suspect's ego was so large it would tolerate hiding only in a place as grandiose as Mt. Aegis.

Vice President Mauve was investigating a profitable tourist attraction (not hiding, she swore).

The person at the Sonic Oscillator did not want a promotion.

The perpetrator was hiding in a place that at least helps you think.

HINT

Executive Eggplant was the suspect who wanted a better job. Any job!

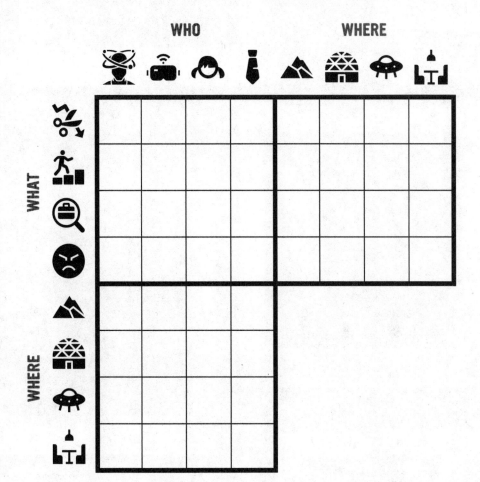

_____ **WHO?**

_____ **WHERE?**

_____ **WHAT?**

Solution to Episode Eight

"It was my dad, as a consequence of cost cutting, and he's in the Sonic Oscillator!"

Olivia raced to the Sonic Oscillator, a giant dome in the middle of the desert, and found her father sitting cross-legged on the floor.

"Dad!" she exclaimed. "Several people have been murdered, and I know it's because of your cost cutting."

"Oh," he said, "that's very unfortunate. Perhaps I cut the costs a little too much. So, you think I should cut back my cutbacks?"

"If it stops people from being murdered, yes, absolutely!"

"Okay, hon. For you, I'll do it. One day, though, you'll inherit the company, and we'll see what you do when you're CEO of TekCo Futures. Maybe you'll make the same decisions that I do."

Olivia did not think that was true, but she understood there were things that her father didn't tell her.

That evening, when Olivia tried to log on to her company computer, she discovered that she was locked out. And even with all her computer knowledge, she couldn't unlock it. So she went to report the issue to the IT guy, and when she got there, he told her, "I've been waiting for you."

He handed her an envelope.

"What is this?" Olivia asked. "Who are you really?"

"It's an envelope, and I'm Deductive Logico."

FINGERPRINTING KIT

MEMBERSHIP CARD

DETECTIVE NOTEBOOK

DECODER RING

DAME OBSIDIAN NOVEL

MYSTERY MIDNIGHT MOVIE

FAKE MUSTACHE

MAGNIFYING GLASS

DECODED

A B C D E F G H I J K L M N O P Q R S T U V W X Y Z
Z Y X W V U T S R Q P O N M L K J I H G F E D C B A

ENCODED

EXHIBIT E:
CONTENTS OF A STANDARD-ISSUE DETECTIVE KIT

THE WHOLE GANG

IN

DISASTER AT DETECTIVE ACADEMY

Deductive Logico had now invited all the detectives to join the Detective Club. But in order for them to call themselves junior detectives, they'd first need to pass some introductory lessons and tests at Detective Academy.

"There's more school?" Jake exclaimed.

"I hope we don't have to learn any logic," Julius said.

Olivia had been about to say, "Wow, that's wonderful! I can't wait to go to Detective Academy and learn all the skills necessary to be a great detective," but when she saw how the others reacted, she decided to bite her tongue.

Instead, the silence was broken by Buster adding his commentary: "Meow."

"Couldn't have said it better myself," Julius replied.

Assistant detectives led them into the Detective Academy and showed them their quarters. Olivia had a cutting-edge computer station. Julius had a collection of crystals. Buster even had a cat bed made especially for him, which he found rather to his liking. Meanwhile, Jake was given a Detective Kit autographed by Logico himself. (It's entered as Exhibit E, at the start of this section.)

Then they got to see the Detective Club Hall of Stolen Goods, where they encountered Techno-Magus Moss's computers, the emerald from Sacred Kidney (the church no longer valued it, now that they knew it was clearly not actually the petrified kidney of a saint), an autographed photograph of Orangutan Orange, and an ancient hard drive containing the last known copy of Maximo 2000. "These are all that remain of the criminal enterprises you all have thwarted. But this doesn't mean you're detectives yet. Tomorrow morning, I'll show you around our facilities and have you all solve a couple of introductory mysteries, both to sharpen your skills and to demonstrate for the senior detectives that you really have what it takes. Do you?"

They all said that they did, but what none of them knew was

that this was not going to be an easy day at school, and they were going to be tested far more than any of them could have ever expected.

Here is the case file known forevermore as *Disaster at Detective Academy*.

EPISODE ONE
WELCOME TO DETECTIVE ACADEMY

"If you want to join the Detective Club, here's the first test!" Deductive Logico said. "There's a bomb hidden somewhere in the Detective Academy!" Everybody screamed. And then Logico clarified, "No, it's a fake bomb. It's a test bomb. But if you can't find it in the next four minutes, we'll all be fake dead. And...go!"

WHERE IS THE BOMB?

FINGERPRINT PRACTICE ROOM

Here you can learn to both take people's fingerprints and match them with the prints they already left.

(SMALL ROOM)

LOGIC CLASSROOM

In this room, you can study the world's greatest crime-fighting technology: logic.

(LARGE ROOM)

LENS-GRINDING WORKSHOP

Here is where the curved lenses for magnifying glasses are made.

(MEDIUM ROOM)

DARKROOM

In the old days, this room was used to develop photos. Now it's used as a quiet place to think.

(SMALL ROOM)

HOW IS IT HIDDEN?

BENEATH A PILE OF PAPERS

The real trick to hiding something is to put something incredibly boring on top of it.

JUST IN THE CORNER

Sometimes the best hiding spot is just an unused corner somewhere.

IN A SAFE

It's hard to break into, but it's not hard to explode out of.

INSIDE A DESK

The easiest part of hiding a bomb is that you don't have to retrieve it.

CLUES & EVIDENCE

There was no desk in the logic classroom.

If the bomb was in the darkroom, it would be hidden in the corner somewhere.

There were absolutely no piles of papers in the fingerprint practice room.

One of the detectives was having trouble piecing together this clue: *T hef in ge rpr intp rac tic ero omd id no tha ʋead es kinit.*

When there was only a minute left, Logico told them the bomb was in a safe!

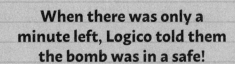

HINT

The clue that was difficult to piece together read: The fingerprint practice room did not have a desk in it.

176 • MURDLE JR.

WHERE

FINGERPRINT PRACTICE ROOM

LOGIC CLASSROOM

LENS-GRINDING WORKSHOP

DARKROOM

HOW

BENEATH A PILE OF PAPERS

JUST IN THE CORNER

IN A SAFE

INSIDE A DESK

_____

WHERE?

_____

HOW?

THE FAKE CASE OF THE FAKE MANSION

In the middle of the Detective Academy, they've built a mystery-mansion set to train the detectives to interrogate witnesses and solve cases. But then someone was fake murdered, and the four junior detectives were asked to solve the case.

WHO IS THE FAKE MURDERER?

ADMIRAL NAVY

He's the son of an Admiral Navy who's the son of an Admiral Navy.

(5'9" • RIGHT-HANDED • BLUE EYES • BROWN HAIR)

DAME OBSIDIAN

The mystery writer agreed to help the junior detectives on the condition that she can write about it.

(5'4" • LEFT-HANDED • GREEN EYES • BLACK HAIR)

DEDUCTIVE LOGICO

Recruiting and training the next generation of detectives is just the logical thing to do.

(6'0" • RIGHT-HANDED • BROWN EYES • BLACK HAIR)

INSPECTOR IRRATINO

He has agreed to participate in the training today as a favor to Logico.

(6'2" • LEFT-HANDED • GREEN EYES • BROWN HAIR)

"It was in the fingerprint practice room, in a safe!"

"Aha!" Logico said, as he picked up the fake bomb. It had a very realistic red digital display, just like bombs in the movies. And it was counting down from 4...3...2...and Logico shut it off. "Just in time! Congratulations, detectives! Now, we move on to our second test."

WHERE DID THEY FAKE MURDER?

THE SECLUDED GROUNDS

Around the fake mansion is about five feet of grass, which ends at the walls of the warehouse.

THE GRAND ENTRANCE

The mansion is built at seventy percent scale, so it's a slightly less grand entrance than it could be.

THE CLOCK ROOM

A room filled with clocks. Every mystery mansion has some weird room like this.

THE GREAT HALL

It's got a roaring fireplace (which is really just a projection, for safety purposes).

A bunch of black hair was
found in the great hall.

A left-handed suspect
was adjusting all the clocks.

Neither the tallest nor the shortest
suspect was at the grand entrance.

The detectives were given a clue written
on a piece of paper, but the letters were
scrambled: DAILRMA AVYN SWA NTO
IN HET GNDRA EETRACNN EERTIH.

The murder had been
committed in front
of a projected fire.

HINT

The scrambled clue says that Admiral Navy was not at the
grand entrance, either.

WHO

 ADMIRAL NAVY

 DAME OBSIDIAN

 DEDUCTIVE LOGICO

 INSPECTOR IRRATINO

WHERE

 THE SECLUDED GROUNDS

 THE GRAND ENTRANCE

 THE CLOCK ROOM

 THE GREAT HALL

_____

WHO?

_____

WHERE?

THE CASE OF THE NOT-DEAD DETECTIVES

Suddenly, all the adult detectives began to fall to the ground, unconscious, and our four junior detectives just managed to lock themselves in the high-security command center. There, they put together everything they knew about the attack, piecing together the clues that they had found and determining which ones were falsely planted.

WHERE WAS THE ATTACK LAUNCHED FROM?

DRAKONIA

Probably one of the scariest places on the planet. Please not here, please not here....

(COUNTRY)

NEW AEGIS

Approximately half of the world's UFO sightings occur in this one town.

(TOWN)

HOLLYWOOD

The glitz! The glamour! The competing movie studios struggling desperately for power!

(TOWN)

THE INVESTIGATION INSTITUTE

The Detective Club has always had the Investigation Institute on its list of Spooky Organizations to Watch.

(NONPROFIT)

Solution to Episode Two

WHAT WERE THE CLUES THAT POINTED THERE?

FOOTPRINTS

One of the most famous clues of all time. Iconic.

A MOVIE CAMERA

You can capture movies on film with this. Or you can hit someone over the head and capture *them*.

```
0110
1001
1010
```

A CODED MESSAGE

It's a series of beeps and boops, but if you translate it, it's actually pretty ominous.

DIGITAL BREADCRUMBS

Buster was disappointed to learn that these were not real breadcrumbs, which are delicious.

The movie camera sure suggested that this was an operation planned in Hollywood.

The series of beeps and boops—when decoded—spelled out a series of letters, which themselves needed to be decoded. The message began, "HITS SI A EEGMSSA MROF THE VAINOTINSETIG SETTTINUI."

The digital breadcrumbs did not suggest that the operation was planned from one of the scariest places on the planet.

The only real clue was the footprints: The rest were all planted!

HINT

The footprints pointed to a place where none of them wanted to go.

WHERE

DRAKONIA

NEW AEGIS

HOLLYWOOD

THE INVESTIGATION INSTITUTE

WHAT

FOOTPRINTS

A MOVIE CAMERA

**0110
1001
1010**
A CODED MESSAGE

DIGITAL BREADCRUMBS

_____

WHERE?

_____

WHAT?

THE DEADLY DRAKONIAN DILEMMA!

When the four junior detectives arrived in Drakonia, they realized that narrowing the origin of the attack down to an entire country still left a whole lot of potential suspects. But an organization must be behind this, and its secret base must be somewhere.

WHO IS BEHIND THIS?

S.P.Y.

Nobody knows what the letters stand for. That's a tightly held secret.

(SECRET AGENCY)

THE RED REVOLUTION

Major Red has launched a revolution in Drakonia, and his agents are traveling the world to sow discord.

(MILITIA MOVEMENT)

THE INVESTIGATION INSTITUTE

The spookiest organization in the world: They investigate the mysteries that other people deem impossible.

(NONPROFIT)

TEKCO FUTURES

They're powerful enough to be behind something like this. But would they? (Yes.)

(FORTUNE 500)

Solution to Episode Three

The attack was launched from Drakonia, and the footprints were the clue that pointed there!

So the four detectives headed off to Drakonia, using the special transportation method available to the members of the Detective Club: buying a regular airline ticket.

(Olivia thought about offering the use of her dad's company jet, before remembering that it had smashed in the desert. And they were not exactly on great terms right now.)

WHERE IS THEIR SECRET BASE?

THE MADDING MOUNTAINS

These are the famous mountains of Drakonian legends, where Castle Eminence sits.

(OUTDOORS)

THE SCREAMING FOREST

The forest doesn't actually scream. Not usually, at least. More of a spooky whisper.

(OUTDOORS)

THE VIOLET ISLES

These are beautiful islands just outside the bay. They're a perfect vacation spot or military outpost.

(OUTDOORS)

THE WESTERN CITADEL

A great tower that's in the middle of the oil fields. Some say it's haunted, but maybe that's just because of all the ghosts.

(INDOORS)

No secret agency was operating out of the Violet Isles.

TekCo Futures had a base of operations in the middle of the oil fields.

No representatives from the Investigation Institute ever heard a spooky whisper (much to their dismay, because they loved spooky whispers).

The Screaming Forest was never home to any agents of S.P.Y.

After careful review, it was clear that the attack had been coordinated from the Madding Mountains!

HINT

The Investigation Institute had set up a well-funded facility in the Violet Isles.

WHO

S.P.Y.

THE RED
REVOLUTION

THE
INVESTIGATION
INSTITUTE

TEKCO FUTURES

WHERE

THE MADDING
MOUNTAINS

THE SCREAMING
FOREST

THE VIOLET
ISLES

THE WESTERN
CITADEL

WHO?

WHERE?

EPISODE FIVE
ESCAPE FROM THE CASTLE DUNGEON

"And that's how we got into this mess," Olivia said, having recounted the entire series of events up until this moment. "Now," she said, oblivious to the fact that her fellow detectives were bored/annoyed by the long monologue they'd already lived through, "we just have to figure out how to escape this dungeon. We'll need the key."

WHO HAS THE KEY?

VISCOUNT EMINENCE

It's technically his castle, so really, he deserves to have the key.

(5'2" • LEFT-HANDED • GRAY EYES • BROWN HAIR)

GUARD GRAY

He is definitely supposed to have the key, and he claims that he does. But does he?

(5'5" • RIGHT-HANDED • BLUE EYES • GRAY HAIR)

DICTIONARY DIRT

Here's another kid detective who tried to take down S.P.Y., and it ended the same way for him. (In the dungeon.)

(4'4" • RIGHT-HANDED • BROWN EYES • BROWN HAIR)

Solution to Episode Four

"It was S.P.V., in the Madding Mountains!"

The four detectives hiked through the Screaming Forest and up the Madding Mountains until they finally stood before Castle Eminence. This is when the events depicted in the "How to Solve" section took place. To refresh your memory, flip back to the beginning to see.

If you want the short version, here it is: They burst into the tower, confronted Agent Apricot, and were immediately thrown into the dungeon. Julius said, "How did we get into this mess?" Then Olivia began retelling everyone's stories. And...well, you know the rest.

WHERE WOULD HE HIDE IT?

IN HIS SHOE

This is an overused hiding spot, perhaps, but it's a classic for a reason.

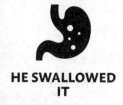

HE SWALLOWED IT

All the detectives hoped it wasn't this one, because getting it back would be...unpleasant.

HE MEMORIZED AND DESTROYED IT

First, you commit the key to memory. Then, when you need it, you rebuild it.

WILL THEY BE ABLE TO ESCAPE?

YES, IN A VERY COOL WAY

Even Olivia (with her insistence on accuracy) would say they could escape.

MAYBE, BUT IN AN EMBARRASSING WAY

They're going to make it out, but they're not going to be happy about it.

NO, THEY WON'T

Uh-oh, kids. It looks like the whole use-the-key strategy might not work out.

CLUES & EVIDENCE

No brown-haired suspect would put the key in their shoe.

Dictionary Dirt would not swallow a key under any circumstances.

If the key was swallowed, then maybe they'd escape, but in an embarrassing way.

If Dictionary Dirt has the key, they will certainly not escape.

Jake solved the case when she realized that the key had been memorized.

HINT

Viscount Eminence would swallow the key. If he hid it, that's how he did it.

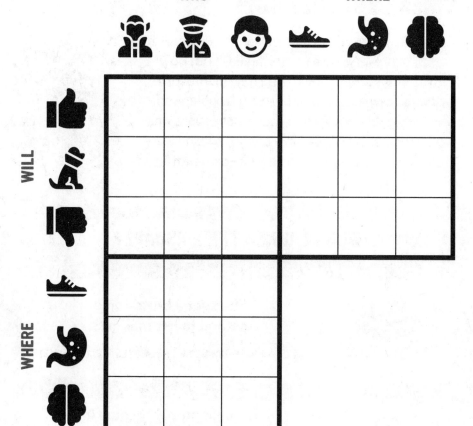

WHO?

WHERE?

WILL?

EPISODE SIX
WHERE DID THEY GO?!

Guard Gray peeked into the cell and realized with horror that everyone had vanished! Oh no, now *he* had a mystery to solve. And if he didn't solve it quickly, he was going to be in big trouble. And, as you might imagine for a mercenary guard who works for a secret agent in a castle, getting in trouble with your boss can be a life-or-death issue.

WHO PLANNED THEIR ESCAPE?

JAKE

She's got a brute-force method to her madness.

(4'2" • RIGHT-HANDED • GREEN EYES • BLOND HAIR)

JULIUS

He could probably come up with a million ways to escape a jail cell, but would any of them work?

(4'4" • LEFT-HANDED • BROWN EYES • BLACK HAIR)

BUSTER McPAWS

They hadn't invented a prison that could hold Buster. Except the prison of hunger.

(1'6" [WITHOUT TAIL] • RIGHT-PAWED • GREEN EYES • BROWN FUR)

OLIVIA

She could calculate the exact chance of any escape method succeeding and then rank the results in descending order of probability.

(4'2" • RIGHT-HANDED • HAZEL EYES • BROWN HAIR)

Solution to Episode Five

"It was Dictionary Dirt, and he had memorized and destroyed the key, and no, we won't be able to escape!"

"What do you mean we won't be able to escape?" Dictionary Dirt said. "You underestimate my cunning! I will simply make a replacement key. All I need are a key-cutting machine and a generous quantity of brass-nickel alloy."

"We don't have any of those!" everybody shouted, including Viscount Eminence. They'd have to find another way out.

WHAT WAS THEIR PLAN?

SOME SORT OF FLYING MACHINE

You'd find a drawing of this in a Renaissance notebook labeled something like FLYCOPTER.

CLASSIC WOODEN CATAPULT

This has the power to launch a bus a mile, so it could definitely throw some kids and a cat.

TRICK THE GUARD

Guard Gray knew this was probably impossible, but he put it on the list anyway.

GETAWAY ALLIGATOR

There's no better vehicle if you want to go fast and eat anything in your way.

WHERE WOULD THE GANG BE NOW?

THE TOWER

This would be bad news for Guard Gray, because his boss would probably fire and/or kill him.

THE GREAT HALL

Hopefully they're not causing trouble in the Great Hall, having a food fight or something.

THE SCREAMING FOREST

Oh no, what if these meddling kids have already escaped to the wilderness?

STILL IN THE CELL

Wait, what?

CLUES & EVIDENCE

Jake suggested something that could launch a bus a mile.

If they'd used Buster's plan, they'd be in the Screaming Forest by now.

If they'd used a getaway alligator, they would *not* still be in the cell.

The escape method straight out of a Renaissance notebook would have taken them straight to the tower.

Olivia wrote down her plan in Detective Code: *DV HSLFOW HGZB RM GSV XVOO.* (See Exhibit E, at the beginning of this section.)

The guard realized too late that he was being tricked!

HINT

Buster wanted to use a getaway alligator, an animal that both terrified and intrigued him.

WHO

WHAT

WHERE

WHAT

_____ WHO?

_____ WHAT?

_____ WHERE?

EPISODE SEVEN
ONE LAST SURPRISE TWIST!

When the four detectives-in-training arrived at the tower, they discovered to their horror that Agent Apricot, the evil villain behind everything, was lying dead on the floor. Somebody must have gotten to her first. But who? And how? And why?

WHO KILLED AGENT APRICOT?

VISCOUNT EMINENCE

"Oh, so I ran up here and murdered someone really quickly before you got here?!"

(5'2" • LEFT-HANDED • GRAY EYES • BROWN HAIR)

EXECUTIVE EGGPLANT

Why is he here? Doesn't he have a job to do at TekCo Futures?

(5'5" • LEFT-HANDED • GREEN EYES • BLACK HAIR)

MRS. RUBY

She's the world's greatest jewel thief. But is she also the world's greatest secret-agent killer?

(5'6" • RIGHT-HANDED • GREEN EYES • RED HAIR)

Solution to Episode Six

WHAT WEAPON DID THEY USE?

A ROBOT CONTROLLED BY MAXIMO 2000

It's an old-timey virus, and it's an old-timey robot, too.

(HEAVYWEIGHT)

A LUCKY PENCIL

Hey, wait a second, is that Sterling's lucky pencil?

(LIGHTWEIGHT)

A GIANT EMERALD

This is easily the most expensive weapon in the book.

(MEDIUM-WEIGHT)

WHERE DID THEY DO IT?

THE BALCONY

It has a beautiful view of the Screaming Forest. You can almost hear the trees screaming!

(OUTDOORS)

THE GIANT MACHINE

It operates on the same principle as the machine from the Investigation Institute, only bigger.

(INDOORS)

THE BIG THRONE

This is a giant throne that the ruler of Drakonia used to sit on.

(INDOORS)

WHY DID THEY DO IT?

S.P.Y.
TO TAKE OVER S.P.Y.

Somebody else wanted to be in charge of S.P.Y., and there's only one way to do it.

TO KICK OUT AN INTRUDER

Honestly, being kicked out is the best-case scenario for a caught intruder.

TO SEE INTO THE FUTURE

Seeing into the future would really help you. Or would it? You'd have to see the future to know for sure.

A beautiful emerald glinted
in the moonlight outdoors.

A lightweight weapon was held by the
person who wanted to see into the future.

Viscount Eminence was reconnecting
with his old-timey robot, which
he'd had since the eighties.

The suspect with black hair
did not want to take over S.P.Y.

The person sitting on the big throne
wanted to kick out an intruder.

The body was draped
over the giant machine.

HINT

Immediately, Jake noticed that Executive Eggplant was
holding Sterling's lucky pencil.

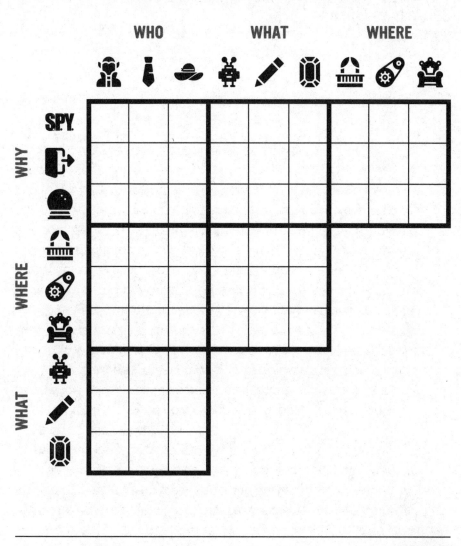

WHO

WHAT

WHERE

WHY

SPY.

WHERE

WHAT

_____ **WHO?**

_____ **WHAT?**

_____ **WHERE?**

_____ **WHY?**

allow us to create a much better one. One in which I rule! No longer will I have to listen to bosses. No longer will you have to steal. We will be masters of our destinies! And rulers of everyone else's!"

Mrs. Ruby looked at him, and at the kids, and down at the emerald. Then, she turned and looked out over the balcony at the Screaming Forest, seemingly miles below, an ocean of trees.

"What are you doing?" Executive Eggplant yelled.

"You don't understand at all," Mrs. Ruby said. "I love stealing."

She pulled back her arm and hurled the emerald off the balcony.

"Noooo!" Eggplant shouted. He raced toward the edge and dove after the emerald, and before he realized what he was doing, he had slipped off the edge and fallen to the ground below.

The four kids raced across the balcony to look, but there was nothing but jagged rocks and pitch-black forest. They couldn't see Eggplant's body at all.

"You'd be surprised how often that happens," Viscount Eminence said. "I really should install some higher railings."

The four kids all thanked Mrs. Ruby for what she had done.

"That emerald was worth millions," Olivia said. "I can't believe that you were willing to throw it off the edge."

"What are you talking about?" Mrs. Ruby said, and she pulled the emerald out of her pocket. "Classic sleight of hand. This is basic thief stuff, children. Better luck next time."

Then she held out her hand, and a rope was lowered into it. The four detectives looked up, and they saw that the rope was connected to a whisper-quiet helicopter, which hovered above them. "Let me give you all another tip, until we meet again: Always have an escape plan."

And then the rope pulled her up and away.

"It was Executive Eggplant, with a lucky pencil, at the giant machine, to see into the future!"

Olivia explained, "Here is how it all ties together! Techno-Magus Moss built a machine that could give her total knowledge, but she was foiled by Julius and Coral and died. But though she passed away and her computers were destroyed, her invention lived on. It just needed a bigger gemstone to work! The Sacred Kidney emerald was definitely big enough to power it, but after Jake uncovered it, it was taken to a top secret vault. Earl Grey heard about the emerald, and he wanted to steal it, so he hired Mrs. Ruby to steal a great ape to steal it. But when Buster McPaws foiled that plot, Mrs. Ruby decided to just steal it herself. And once she had it, she sold it to the only people who could afford to buy such an expensive emerald, my father's company, TekCo Futures."

Executive Emerald was outraged. "We put every penny into this project! We cut every other program. But you ruined it! You made your father weak! And when the Detective Club confiscated the evidence, we had to hire S.P.Y. to break into the Detective Academy and steal it back. But unfortunately, we brought you tiny tattle-tales with us, too."

"Junior detectives!" Jake corrected.

"It doesn't matter what you are! You're not going to stop me from turning on this machine, just like Agent Apricot couldn't stop me! She wouldn't go along with my plan, so I had to do her in!"

"Don't you understand?" Julius cried. "You'll destroy the world by doing that!" He did not mention the Entity he had spoken with on the astral plane, because he knew adults had a way of dismissing anything you learned in a vision or a dream.

"Give me the emerald!" Executive Eggplant called out to Mrs. Ruby. "I can use it to start the machine right now! When I rule the world, I will give you riches beyond belief."

But Mrs. Ruby did not give him the emerald. Instead, she asked him a question: "Is what they say true? Will it really destroy the world?"

"It'll destroy the current world," Eggplant replied. "But it will

THE ANSWER AT THE END OF IT ALL

Finally, in the tower atop Castle Eminence, the four detectives stood on the balcony and looked out at the forest below. "That's not all," Olivia said. "Someone else was behind this. Someone put the pieces into motion. Had us sent here. My calculations prove it."

WHO WAS SECRETLY BEHIND IT ALL?

HAZEL

They haven't seen the last of Olivia's rival.

(4'3" • LEFT-HANDED • HAZEL EYES • BROWN HAIR)

MRS. RUBY

She's an internationally infamous jewel thief. But maybe she's set her sights even higher.

(5'6" • RIGHT-HANDED • GREEN EYES • RED HAIR)

DEDUCTIVE LOGICO

He seems like a nice, logical-minded guy. Could that all be a mask to hide his devious nature?

(6'0" • RIGHT-HANDED • BROWN EYES • BLACK HAIR)

WHERE IS THEIR REAL HEADQUARTERS?

DETECTIVE CLUB

Was this whole operation just run out of the Detective Club? Are they still on a set?

(INDOORS)

PIRATE COVE

This is where all the criminals and thieves hang out and have parties.

(OUTDOORS)

A LUXURY TREEHOUSE

A really cool place to spend an afternoon with your friends, so long as your friends are birds.

(INDOORS)

WHAT WAS THEIR SECRET PLAN?

TO TEST THESE FOUR DETECTIVES

Sometimes, to become a junior detective, you need to be tested.

TO CREATE A HUGE DISTRACTION

This means that as bad as all of this was, something worse was going on.

TO TAKE OVER THE WORLD

Honestly, who could tolerate the stress of running the entire world?

WHY DID THEY DO IT?

TO BE READY FOR WHAT'S TO COME

If you know what's coming, you can prepare for it. If you don't, uh-oh!

BECAUSE OF A DEEP INNER INSECURITY

Sometimes, when you don't believe in yourself, you do wild things to compensate.

ONCE AGAIN, MONEY

This is one of the most popular motivations, because it's shared by everybody.

A left-handed suspect wanted
to take over the world.

Mrs. Ruby wanted to create a huge distraction.

Nobody was trying to test these four detectives
from their HQ in a luxury treehouse.

A single black hair was found indoors.

The suspect with a secret plan to take over the
world would do it because of a deep insecurity.

The person who would have done it
for (once again) money was outdoors.

**The whole operation was
motivated by a desire to
prepare for what's to come.**

HINT

Unfortunately, we can't authorize any hints on this last one.

WHO   WHERE   WHAT

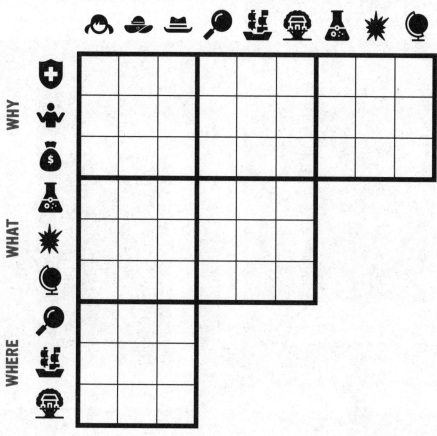

WHO?

WHERE?

WHAT?

WHY?

Solution to Episode Eight

"It was Deductive Logico, at the Detective Club, to test these four detectives, to prepare for what's to come!"

"Wait!" Jake said. "So this whole thing was a test?"

"Yes," Logico replied, "and congratulations. You passed."

"But were the murders real?"

"Oh yes," Logico said. "Those weren't part of the plan. You actually solved real murders."

"And was the machine to see into the future real?"

"Oh yes, that was real, too."

"Was S.P.Y. an actual organization, then? Or just a front?"

"No, they're very much real, and they're very much behind it all."

"Then what part was faked?" Olivia asked.

"Oh, hmm....," Logico said. "I didn't really pass out at the attack on the Detective Club. I held my breath!"

DETECTIVE EXAM

Now that you've finished the book, you're ready to take your Detective Exam! Now, don't worry, because the purpose of this exam is not to grade you. None of these questions has a right answer. Instead, they are meant to help you determine what kind of detective you are.

This will help you hone your mystery-solving talents and figure out how to specialize when you join the Detective Club as a junior member.

1. Which of these subjects do you like the most?
   A. P.E.
   B. Art or English
   C. History
   D. Math

2. Which of these field trips sounds the most exciting?
   A. Visiting a big city
   B. Hiking in the woods
   C. Checking out a zoo
   D. Going to a museum

3. There's a snow day. What do you do?

    A. Obviously a snowball fight

    B. Build a snowman

    C. Enjoy a nice cup of hot chocolate

    D. Study the weather patterns to see if tomorrow will be one, too

4. If you suspected somebody was a murderer, what would you do?

    A. Confront them immediately and see how they react

    B. See how that accusation feels in your gut

    C. Spy on them and see what they're up to—murderer stuff?

    D. Collect as much evidence against them as possible before coming to a judgment

5. What's your favorite sandwich?

    A. Grilled cheese

    B. PB&J

    C. Tuna

    D. Depends on the bread

6. If you were given a million dollars, what would you spend it on?

    A. A tank

    B. A hedge maze

    C. An endless amount of toys

    D. A top-of-the-line computer system

7. If you saw a penguin in the park, what would you do?

    A. Check if you were being recorded

    B. Go up to him and try to befriend him

    C. Be very cautious—this penguin might be up to
       something

    D. Try to figure out where this penguin's supposed to be

8. An ideal fort would contain which of the following?

    A. Booby traps for intruders

    B. Séance room

    C. Telescope/periscope

    D. Lots and lots of books

9. What are your favorite topics for a nonfiction book?

    A. Survival and how-to

    B. Animals and magic

    C. History and biographies

    D. Science and technology

10. Which of these answers seems the most appealing?

    A. This one, obviously

    B. Maybe this one (maybe not)

    C. Hmm…interesting

    D. All the answers are equally appealing

IF YOU ANSWERED MORE As

You're a Gumshoe, like Jake. You march out into the field, interrogate the suspects, confront the culprit, and crack the case. You're not afraid to get your hands dirty—or your face, for that matter. Sure, the life of a Gumshoe is dangerous, but you wouldn't have it any other way.

IF YOU ANSWERED MORE Bs

You're an Intuitive, like Julius. You feel out the vibes and follow your gut to solve the mystery. You're not afraid to act on a hunch. Sure, you might not be able to use evidence you got from a crystal ball in court, but that doesn't mean you can't use it as a starting point.

IF YOU ANSWERED MORE Cs

You're a Snoop, like Buster McPaws. You know how to sneak around and watch from the shadows. You know that often, as a detective, getting too close to the suspects makes it hard for you to see the full picture. Instead of barging in and demanding answers, you wait and let them reveal themselves to you.

IF YOU ANSWERED MORE Ds

You're a Consultant, like Olivia. You take in all the facts and the data for the case and compute it all before deciding whodunit. Some people say that a Consultant can't possibly solve a crime without actually visiting the crime scene. But those people, statistically, don't have the mental powers needed to be a Consultant.

CONGRATULATIONS, DETECTIVE!

MAKING IT TO THE END OF THIS BOOK PROVES THAT YOU HAVE what it takes to become a junior detective. Now you're fully qualified to fill out the following Detective Club ID Card. Congratulations, junior detective, you've earned it!

Sincerely,

Deductive Logico

DETECTIVE CLUB
MEMBERSHIP CARD

Name —————————————

Date Joined —————————————

Detective Type —————————————

This card entitles its holder to
investigate mysteries wherever they lead.

FULL SOLUTIONS

JAKE IN *THE CASE OF THE MISSING PENCIL*

EPISODE ONE: YOU CAN'T SPELL *CRIME* WITHOUT A PENCIL, PAGE 25

Rose | the fort
Daisy | the slide
Brick | the swings

EPISODE TWO: THE WRITE WAY TO FIND A PENCIL, PAGE 29

Miss Saffron's desk | creating a huge distraction
Brick's cubby | being really quiet and sneaky
the ferret cage | loudly confronting Brick about it

EPISODE THREE: THE MYSTERY UNFOLDS, PAGE 33

the new janitor | the dumpster outside
Coach Raspberry Jr. | the janitorial closet
Daisy | the trash can in the hallway
Sister Lapis | the principal's office

EPISODE FOUR: THE GROSS CASE OF THE GARBAGE CAN, PAGE 37

a used tissue | it's actually *behind* the trash can
a manila envelope | sitting on the top
wrapped in a banana peel | somewhere in the middle
just loose | buried on the bottom

EPISODE FIVE: THE SENTENCING OF DETECTIVE JAKE, PAGE 41

hanging out in the halls | not that serious | after-school detention

going through the garbage | depends on how often you do it | sit by the fence during recess

disrespecting the nuns | very, very serious | potential expulsion

EPISODE SIX: THE CASE OF THE OVERHEARD ARREST, PAGE 45

Coach Raspberry Jr. | *the* **Sacred Kidney | the chapel**

Principal Applegreen | a letter | janitorial closet

Mrs. Ruby | a big bunch of cash | the only cafeteria in the school

EPISODE SEVEN: THE CASE OF THE MISSING JAKE, PAGE 49

Jake | the principal's office | two words: *ventilation system*

Principal Applegreen | the boiler room | not trying to hide at all

Sister Lapis | the chapel | being super still and silent

Officer Copper | the steps out front | wearing a ridiculous mustache

EPISODE EIGHT: THE END OF THE SCRIBBLED LINE, PAGE 53

Brick | the ferret | reckless driving

Principal Applegreen | Raspberry's letter | selling off the school's relics

Miss Saffron | a big bunch of cash | violation of zoning laws

Jake | *the* Sacred Kidney | generally being a bully

JULIUS IN *THE MYSTERY OF THE UNIVERSE*

EPISODE ONE: WHO SENT THE SECRET NOTE?, PAGE 63

Uncle Irratino | the Grand Chateau
Numerologist Night | the impossible hedge maze
Coral | the observation tower

EPISODE TWO: WHERE IS NUMEROLOGIST NIGHT?, PAGE 67

the upside-down fountain | take only lefts
the center of the maze | take all rights
the lonely tower | alternate taking lefts and rights

EPISODE THREE: THE SECRET CASE OF THE SECRET, PAGE 71

a smuggling operation | the attic
an unlicensed zoo | the balcony
a private laboratory | the parlor
a literal gold mine | the president's office

EPISODE FOUR: THE ROOM WITH FOUR SECRET PASSAGES, PAGE 75

the bookshelf | a small wooden button on the floor
the fireplace | pulling a candlestick from the wall
the grandfather clock | taking a certain book off the shelf
a portrait | knocking on the mantel

EPISODE FIVE: THE SECRET OF THE SECRET LAB, PAGE 79

Alchemist Raven | your classic alchemy lab | winning the lottery
Cryptozoologist Cloud | a potions and poisons lab | immortality
Techno-Magus Moss | a computer lab | total knowledge

EPISODE SIX: THE GREATEST ESCAPE, PAGE 83

Uncle Irratino | the Grand Chateau basement | a really good memory
Coral | the deep dark woods | a map and compass
Numerologist Night | even deeper into the tunnels | a phone

EPISODE SEVEN: A MYSTERY ON THE ASTRAL PLANE, PAGE 87

Coral | a mountaintop | a lance of emotion
Techno-Magus Moss | the happy meadow | negative thoughts
The Entity | the cosmic void | infinite chaos
Numerologist Night | a big puffy cloud | a dream sword

EPISODE EIGHT: THE MYSTERY OF THE INVESTIGATION INSTITUTE, PAGE 91

Dr. Seashell, D.D.S. | the great gates | they are actually siblings
Coral | the observation tower | to stop the end of the world
Numerologist Night | the impossible hedge maze | to make a whole heap of money
Uncle Irratino | the Grand Chateau | because they were so, so bored

BUSTER McPAWS IN *THE CRIME OF THE CENTURY*

EPISODE ONE: OPERATION: FUR-ENSICS!, PAGE 101

Romeo Raccoon | going through the cat door
Old Man Mint | using the rake as a grabby thing
Clay | a garage door opener

EPISODE TWO: THE CAT BURGLAR STRIKES!, PAGE 105

the front door | secret disguise
the chimney | climbing a tree
the basement window | squeeze mode

EPISODE THREE: SNEAKING THROUGH THE MANSION, PAGE 109

Mrs. Ruby | the basement
Buddy the Dog | the courtyard
Old Man Mint | the grand entrance
an unknown fourth person | the locked upstairs room

EPISODE FOUR: THE MYSTERY BEHIND THE LOCKED DOOR, PAGE 113

another cat | found in the creek
a trained orangutan | kidnapped from the circus
the president of Drakonia | a cardboard box with cheese under it
an evil murderer | broken out of jail

EPISODE FIVE: THE CASE OF THE CIRCUS CAGE, PAGE 117

Old Man Mint | the hall of mirrors | your classic getaway van
Mrs. Ruby | the cages | a giant crane
Kid Khaki | the big top | the magic disappearing assistant trick

EPISODE SIX: THE CASE OF THE COMPROMISED WITNESS, PAGE 121

Mrs. Ruby | the street | the ol' one-two
Old Man Mint | the creek | Tired-Eyes Tea
Mail Carrier Marzipan | Clay's house | a big bag

EPISODE SEVEN: THE CASE OF THE RESCUED PET HUMAN, PAGE 125

Buddy the Dog | slobbering over everything | some kind of evil plan
Mail Carrier Marzipan | one word: *explosives* | the mail must not be stopped
Orangutan Orange | terrifying the kidnappers | to sleep easy at night
Romeo Raccoon | lightning-fast reflexes | mercenary work is always well paid

OLIVIA IN *THE CASE OF THE CORRUPT COMPUTER*

EPISODE FOUR: THE MYSTERY OF THE MISSING KID, PAGE 151

Drakonia | a prearranged stretch limo
New Aegis | a jetpack
a nice English village | a really long secret tunnel
the S.P.Y. satellite | a prototype teleportation machine

EPISODE FIVE: A DEADLY EXECUTIVE DECISION, PAGE 155

Executive Eggplant | their wits | the passenger cabin
Executive Assistant Olive | a parachute | the cockpit
Executive Producer Steel | a bazooka | the wing

EPISODE SIX: THE CASE OF THE CRASHING PLANE, PAGE 159

the navigation software | debugging the code | a flash drive
automatic seat ejector | by tightening some bolts | a mini safety wrench Olivia always carries
the bathroom | she can't | an in-flight magazine

EPISODE SEVEN: EXECUTIVE INDECISION, PAGE 163

Executive Eggplant | a glass dagger | the big cactus
Executive Producer Steel | another in-flight magazine | the wrecked jet
Executive Assistant Olive | a briefcase full of cash | the lush oasis
a desert hermit | a bag of sand | the jagged rock

EPISODE EIGHT: THE BIG FINISH IN NEW AEGIS, PAGE 167

The Big Boss | the Sonic Oscillator | just a consequence of cost cutting
Vice President Mauve | the UFO crash site | to get a better job somewhere else
Hazel | Mt. Aegis | getting revenge on Olivia specifically
Executive Eggplant | the kitschy restaurant | to get a promotion

THE WHOLE GANG IN
DISASTER AT DETECTIVE ACADEMY

EPISODE ONE: WELCOME TO DETECTIVE ACADEMY, PAGE 177

fingerprint practice room | in a safe
logic classroom | beneath a pile of papers
lens-grinding workshop | inside a desk
darkroom | just in the corner

EPISODE TWO: THE FAKE CASE OF THE FAKE MANSION, PAGE 181

Admiral Navy | the secluded grounds
Dame Obsidian | the great hall
Deductive Logico | the grand entrance
Inspector Irratino | the clock room

EPISODE THREE: THE CASE OF THE NOT-DEAD DETECTIVES, PAGE 185

Drakonia | footprints
New Aegis | digital breadcrumbs
Hollywood | a movie camera
the Investigation Institute | a coded message

EPISODE FOUR: THE DEADLY DRAKONIAN DILEMMA!, PAGE 189

S.P.Y. | the Madding Mountains
The Red Revolution | the Screaming Forest
The Investigation Institute | the Violet Isles
TekCo Futures | the Western Citadel

EPISODE FIVE: ESCAPE FROM THE CASTLE DUNGEON, PAGE 193

Viscount Eminence | he swallowed it | maybe, but in an embarrassing way
Guard Gray | in his shoe | yes, in a very cool way
Dictionary Dirt | he memorized and destroyed it | no, they won't

EPISODE SIX: WHERE DID THEY GO?!, PAGE 197

Jake | classic wooden catapult | the Great Hall
Julius | some sort of flying machine | the tower
Buster McPaws | getaway alligator | the Screaming Forest
Olivia | trick the guard | still in the cell

EPISODE SEVEN: ONE LAST SURPRISE TWIST!, PAGE 203

Viscount Eminence | a robot controlled by Maximo 2000 | the big throne | to kick out an intruder
Executive Eggplant | a lucky pencil | the giant machine | to see into the future
Mrs. Ruby | a giant emerald | the balcony | to take over S.P.Y.

EPISODE EIGHT: THE ANSWER AT THE END OF IT ALL, PAGE 211

Hazel | a luxury treehouse | to take over the world | because of a deep inner insecurity
Mrs. Ruby | pirate cove | to create a huge distraction | once again, money
Deductive Logico | Detective Club | to test these four detectives | to be ready for what's to come

ACKNOWLEDGMENTS

If you're interested in writing a book of your own, you should know that a lot of work goes into it from a lot of people who aren't the author.

You need a great editor, which I have in Liz Kossnar. And that editor needs a great assistant, which she has in Lauren Kisare. But to even get to that point you usually need an even greater agent, which I also have: Melissa Edwards at Stonesong.

I would like to thank everyone at Profile Books, including Cindy Chan and Lily Evans, for everything they have done for Murdle, and to Angie Curzi, whose marketing campaign helped put it on the map in the UK.

I'd also like to thank Neil Swaab for designing the cover of this book, as well as the interior. Without his work, it would not look nearly as beautiful. And I'd like to thank all the people who helped me write and test it.

Finally, I would like to thank my girlfriend, Dani Messerschmidt. She's been really wonderful to me for many years, and I could not have written a word of this without her help. (She also designed the exhibits!)

PS: If you're ever in LA, eat at Tara's Himalayan Cuisine. The garlic tofu fueled the writing of this book and certainly many others.

Annie Lesser

G. T. KARBER

grew up in a small town in Arkansas, the son of a judge and a civil rights attorney. Now he is a mystery writer, computer programmer, and the creator of Murdle, the *USA Today* and #1 *Sunday Times* bestselling murder-mystery puzzle book series, available in more than thirty languages. He lives in Los Angeles with Dani Messerschmidt and their two cats, who love to solve the mystery of what's for dinner.

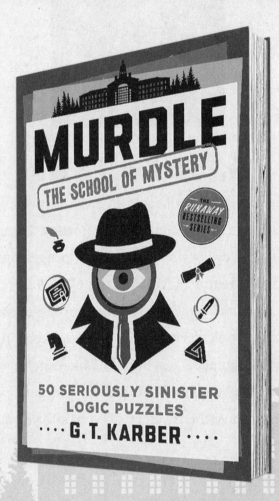